The Essence of Superfine Gold

A Guide on the Stages of the Path to Enlightenment

The Third Dalai Lama

Translator: Dr. Chok Tenzin Monlam

Published in commemoration of the 2550th Mahaparinirvana anniversary of Buddha Shakyamuni

LIBRARY OF TIBETAN WORKS & ARCHIVES

First Edition: March 2007

ISBN: 81-86470-60-3

Published by Library of Tibetan Works & Archives, Dharamsala and printed at VEE EEN PRINT-O-PAC, A-5, Flatted Factory Complex, Okhla Industrial Estate, Ph-III, New Delhi-110020

Contents

Translator's Note

In January 2005, at the request of Geshe Pema Dorjee, Director of Bodong Research and Publication Centre, Dharamsala, I translated Je Tsongkhapa's *Lam rim nyams mgur* (*A Song of Experience*) for him. In April that year – while I was in Kuala Lumpur, Malaysia, as a translator for Lobsang Drakpa Buddhist Centre – I was invited to Singapore to be translator at the teachings of the Venerable Lungrik Namgyal Rinpoche, the hundred-and-first Gaden Throne Holder. While back in Dharamsala I made a rough translation into English of the Third Dalai Lama's famous text, *Lam rim gser zhun ma*, before going on to Singapore and acting as Rinpoche's oral translator for two months. Out of these translations the text grew further.

In December 2006 I joined the Library of Tibetan Works and Archives as head of the Research and Translation Department. In this new capacity it occurred to me that since His Holiness the Fourteenth Dalai Lama was to give teachings from the Third Dalai Lama's seminal text after the Monlam Prayer Festival in March 2007, it might be helpful for the English-speaking section of his audience to be able to refer to a close translation.

Our Director, Geshe Lhakdor, approved my translation and advised me to improve the work which led to me referring to five different versions of this Tibetan text available in our Library. It is upon my critical edition which I then produced this English text that, titled *The Essence of Superfine Gold*. While His Holiness the Third Dalai Lama composed the text in very accessible, colloquial Tibetan, it was a great challenge for me to translate it in so everyday a style.

I am very happy to include here a brief biography of the Third Dalai Lama, *A Song of Experience* by Je Tsongkhapa, along with my critical edition of the Tibetan text.

I dedicate all the merit accumulated from this work to the long life of His Holiness the Fourteenth Dalai Lama and to the people who are working today in every corner of the globe to bring peace, harmony and wellbeing to our Mother Earth. I apologize to the readers for any mistakes found in my translation and invite your valuable suggestions for further improving and refining the contents for any future edition.

Acknowledgements

I must express my deepest gratitude to my friend Tenzin Tsepak and acknowledge that this title is as much his work as mine. Without his painstaking efforts in sitting beside me and comparing my translation with my critical edition of the Tibetan text, this English edition of *The Essence of Superfine Gold* would not be as close as it must be to the words and spirit of the Third Dalai Lama's work. I express my thanks to Julie Morren for editing the initial draft of the English translation. My thanks also go to my friend Jane Perkins for further making the translation comprehensible and accessible, and to Matthew Akester for excellent suggestions in translation.

My heartfelt thanks go to the Library's Director, Geshe Lhakdor, for his valuable guidance at various stages of the critical editing of the Tibetan text and proofreading it and Naga Sangye Tandar ably edited the title's brief biography of the Third Dalai Lama in Tibetan.

A Brief Biography of the Third Dalai Lama

In the year 1543 the Third Dalai Lama, Sonam Gyatso, was born in the village of Upper Khangsar, in the Toelung Valley near Lhasa, to his father Depa Namgyal Dakpa and his mother Pelzom Bhuti. During the time of birth the sky was filled with rainbows and divine beings showered flowers from the heavens. He emerged from the womb still wrapped in his protective amnion which then broke open like a lotus blossoming in the sun.

As soon as he was born his parents gave him the milk of a white goat while reciting auspicious prayers and named him Ranu Sichoe Pelzangpo, meaning "The Glorious and Noble Banisher of Spirits Who Drink Goats' Milk". Right there, at his birth, he recited the six-syllable mantra of Avalokiteshvara.

During his early years, unlike ordinary children he showed many extraordinary signs exhibited by noble beings such as folding his hands in the teaching-giving gesture and assuming meditative postures while sitting. Around the age of three he remembered his previous life as Gedun Gyatso and announced that he was his reincarnation. Accordingly, he became widely acknowledged as the reincarnation of the Second Dalai Lama-to-be, Gedun Gyatso.

At the age of four he started learning to read and write Tibetan and was installed upon the golden throne of Gaden Phodrang Labrang at Drepung Monastery, near Lhasa. He received his full layman's vows of *upasaka* from Panchen Sonam Dakpa (1478–1554) and was ceremonially given the name Sonam Gyatso Palzangpo Tenpai Nyima Chokley Namgyal (The Glorious Ocean of Merit, the Sun of the Teaching that is Victorious in All Directions).

When Sonam Gyatso was five he visited the Choekhor Gyal Monastery at Metok Thang, which he had founded in his previous life in the vicinity of the "Lake of Visions". During this visit the female protectress, Palden Lhamo, performed various miracles to express her delight in him. Sonam Gyatso recited prayers, made offerings and gave teachings to the monks before returning to Drepung.

At seven Sonam Gyatso received the *sramanerika* vows of a novice monk and the Amitayus initiation of long life from Panchen Sonam Dakpa. From Lingtoe Choeje Lekpai Dhondup and Shartse Choeje Lekpa Dhondup he received many profound transmissions of the Sutra and Tantra teachings, which he studied, reflected on and practiced. He began to reside alternately at Choekhor Gyal and Drepung monasteries, and while journeying between the two he gave teachings at monasteries along the way. By this tender age Sonam Gyatso had recited 1,300,000 mantras of Amitayus; 5,000,000 mantras of Saraswati and 400,000 refuge prayers.

In 1552, when he was ten years old, Sonam Gyatso became the twelfth abbot of Drepung. The next year he presided over the Monlam Prayer Festival, convened at Lhasa, where in the mornings he read stories from the Thirty-Four Buddhacharita written by Ashvaghosha and in the afternoons led the congregation in special aspirational and dedication prayers for both the dead and living. Thus he maintained the great legacy of Je Tsongkhapa – founder of Lhasa's Great Monlam Prayer Festival in 1409. During the festival, gods and goddesses showed miraculous signs of their delight in him by releasing a heavy rain of flowers. By the time Sonam Gyatso was eleven he had completed 20,000,000 recitations of the mantra of the Wrathful Form of Guru Padmasambhava. At thirteen he moved to his monastic seat at Choekhor Gyal and completed 100,000 recitations of the mantra of the Black Garuda Wisdom Deity. Then at Drepung he recited the Migtsema Prayer of Je Tsongkhapa 400,000 times.

In 1556, at only fourteen, Sonam Gyatso was able to resolve a serious conflict that had erupted between the rulers of Nedong and the administrative officials of Chongye, since he had already won everybody's trust. In 1558, when he was sixteen he became the thirteenth abbot of Sera Monastery, and the following year Tashi Dakpa Gyaltsan – the great ruler of Nedong – offered him the title of Kanding Tai Gushri Hung Khan and presented him with a red seal accompanied by an edict empowering him to use it. Two years later there was a disastrous flood in Lhasa following heavy rains. So in 1562 Sonam Gyatso initiated the annual custom during the Monlam Prayer Festival of monks adding rocks to the embankment at Lhasa's Kyichu River which protects the sacred Jokhang temple.

In 1564, when he reached twenty-one, Sonam Gyatso took the vows of a *bhikshu* – a fully-ordained monk – from Trichen Gelek Palzang of Dewachen. He then went on to study a wealth of teachings and classic Buddhist texts of philosophy and practice under the tutelage of spiritual masters such as Kunzang Tsepa, Tsarchen Losel Gyatso – a great master of the Sakya tradition – and the Master of Dewachen, Trichen Gelek Palzang.

In 1567, when he was twenty-nine, the lamas of Tashi Lhunpo Monastery invited Sonam Gyatso to the Tsang region of Tibet. Accordingly, he went there and gave many teachings to the monks and lay people. Two years later he ordered the building of images representing the Outer, Inner and Secret Dharma Protectors at Choekhor Gyal monastic seat.

In this way he worked untiringly for Buddhism, visiting most places in the U and Tsang regions of Central Tibet. He kindled faith in those who had no belief in the teachings of the Buddha and increased devotion among the faithful. He primarily resided at both Drepung and Gyal monasteries, regarding these two equally as his monastic seats, taking care of their welfare, proffering Dharma and working to meet their material needs.

In 1574, at the age of thirty-two, Sonam Gyatso founded the Phende Leksheling College known now as Namgyal Dratsang Monastery. Two years later the most powerful khan among Mongols, Altan Khan (1507-1582), invited him to his capital. Before setting out himself he first sent his envoy, Choeje Tsondu Zangpo, who was a Master of Vinaya. In the following year, acquiescing to the persistent requests of Altan Khan, he finally embarked on the journey to the northern land of Mongolia with the wish to propagate Buddhism there.

En route, as Sonam Gyatso was riding by Radeng Monastery, Lord Tashi Rabten approached him, held his mount by the reins and spontaneously said: "I pray for your long life, O glorious Master of the Teaching! May the upholders of the Dharma fill the entire world!" Having said these two lines, the aristocrat shed tears, which so choked him that he could not finish his prayer. Sonam Gyatso, still mounted, replied: "As a benefactor of the Dharma, may your power and wealth increase! And may circumstances that are auspicious for the Dharma long endure!" And thus this popular prayer became known for its profundity of meaning and richness in blessings.

As Sonam Gyatso reached the Drichu River in eastern Kham province, evil spirits started to disturb the water, making it difficult for the travellers and animals to cross. He cast a fierce glance while extending his hand in the gesture of wrath; instantly the troubled water became calm and everyone was able to safely ford the river. Eventually Sonam Gyatso reached the Upper Nyatso region, where he was greeted by a large crowd of followers of the local monastery, who presented him with numerous offerings, including three-thousand gold coins. To this gathering he transmitted the Guru Yoga practice and the six-syllable mantra of Avalokiteshvara. That day alone, almost a thousand people took vows of renunciation and *bhikshu* ordination and were led on the path to liberation.

When Sonam Gyatso camped beside the mighty Machu or Yellow River, many Tibetans who had joined his entourage became fearful, doubting whether they would be able to cross this huge stretch of water. The next morning, however, they were stunned to find that the river was only knee-deep. Carrying on with their journey, they reached Karpo Thang of Arik where the citizens offered Sonam Gyatso a thousand horses and nearly ten thousand cattle and other offerings. There, as a rainbow tent spontaneously manifested, and a rain of divine flowers showered out of the sky, Sonam Gyatso planted the seed of liberation in everyone's mind. Then Choeje Tsondu Zangpo – whom Sonam Gyatso had already appointed as Principal Tutor to Altan Khan – and the translator Gushri, led a convoy of five hundred horsemen to escort him to the Mongolian ruler's palace.

So finally, in 1578, at the age of thirty-six and two years after setting out on his journey to Mongolia, Sonam Gyatso encountered the religious-minded Mongolian khan and thereby became the spiritual guide to Altan Khan. His royal disciple then offered him a golden crown, an act of devotion witnessed by envoys from many lands.

The great khan also offered a vase symbolizing long life, the five symbols of the five Buddha families, and a golden seal fashioned from a hundred gold coins and inscribed with the words: "The Victorious Seal of the Vajradhara Dalai Lama!" and "Dalai Lama Vajradhara", thus honoring him with the title: "Pervasive Lord Vajradhara, the Diamond-bearing Buddha. Since this moment all successive Dalai Lamas have been known by this Mongolian title. In return, the newly-named Dalai Lama bestowed the title "Religious King, the Brahma of Gods" on Altan Khan and began teaching extensively throughout the Mongolian lands. The Third Dalai Lama ordained hundreds of Mongols as monks and nuns and discouraged the sacrificing of animals in Mongolia.

In 1580, at the age of thirty-eight, while journeying home to Lhasa, the Third Dalai Lama sat on the throne of Jangsem Choeje at the Gaden Thupten Choekhor Ling Monastery in Lithang, Kham province, and bestowed extensive teachings on the monastic and lay gathering. He also visited Kubum Jampa Ling Monastery in Amdo province and taught there extensively. At forty-one, as he was visiting Kubum – the sacred birthplace of Je Tsongkhapa – he gave instructions that a center for the study of Buddhism should be founded there. That year Altan Khan died. But only four years later, in 1584, at the invitation of Altan Khan's son and heir,

Dugureng Sengge, the Third Dalai Lama returned to Mongolia to resolve a domestic conflict and generate peace in the land. In the following year he visited Sechen Taiji's land and founded Phuntsok Dhargyal Ling Monastery.

The Third Dalai Lama composed this commentary, *The Essence of Superfine Gold*, as a guide on the stages of the path to enlightenment to benefit the seekers among future generations of humanity. In his rather brief lifetime he also wrote many other praises, spiritual songs of experience and other inspiring compositions.

In 1588, when he was forty-six, the Dalai Lama passed away at Khara Ching in Mongolia. His ashes were then taken back to Drepung Monastery, near Lhasa, where they were enshrined in a silver *stupa*.

A Song of Experience
The Condensed Meaning of Lamrim

Je Tsongkhapa

I bow down my head to the chief of the Shakyas
Whose body was formed through millions of perfect virtues
Whose speech fulfills the hopes of limitless beings
And whose mind sees all objects of knowledge precisely
as they are.

I prostrate to Ajita and Manjughosha
The excellent sons of the peerless Teacher
Who, displaying emanations in the countless realms
Carry out all the tasks of the buddhas.

I bow at the feet of Nagarjuna and Asanga, the Ornaments
of the World
Who are renowned throughout the three realms
And correctly interpreted the Mother of the Victors
Which are so difficult to fathom.

I bow to Dipamkara, the holder of the treasury of instructions
The distilled essence, unmistaken and complete
On the paths of the profound view and vast deeds
Which were well transmitted from the two great refounders.

I respectfully pay homage to the spiritual masters
Who, with skillful deeds moved by compassion
Open the eyes of the fortunate ones to see all the vast scriptures
And the brilliant gateway leading to liberation.

The stages of the path to enlightenment
Have been transmitted in succession through Nagarjuna
and Asanga
The crowning jewels of the learned ones of the world
Whose banner of renown rises high amongst all beings.
As it fulfills every aspiration of sentient beings
It is the king of wish-fulfilling gems of instruction
As it combines the thousand streams of noble teachings
It is also an ocean of glorious, excellent explanations.

It makes one realize that the entire teaching is consistent
It makes one see the entire teaching as spiritual instruction
It makes one discover the intent of the Buddha with ease
And it also saves one from the abyss of grave misdeeds.
Hence, which intelligent being would not be enthralled
By the Stages of the Path of the Three Beings
The excellent instruction relied upon by the many
fortunate beings
The learned ones of India and Tibet?

As the essence of the entire scripture is herein condensed
Even listening to or explaining this teaching once
Certainly accumulates a great virtue of teaching or listening
To the holy Dharma; hence, contemplate on this meaning.

To fulfill all ideal conditions for the good of this
and future lives
The root lies in our spiritual masters, the guides on our path.
Seeing this, follow them properly in thought and deed
Forsaking them not even at the cost of your life
And please them with the offering of practice –
heeding their words.

I, a yogi, practiced in this way.
You, who seek liberation, should do likewise.

This opportune life surpasses a wish-fulfilling gem
Such is found only once this time
So hard to obtain, yet so easy to lose, like a flash of lightning!
Seeing this nature, discard all worldly activities
Just like winnowing the chaff
And, day and night, make it meaningful.
I, a yogi, practiced in this way.
You, who seek liberation, should do likewise.

You are unsure about your birth in the unfortunate realms after death
And certain that the Three Jewels are the protectors from this terror.
So, make your practice of refuge firm
And let not the precepts of your refuge weaken.
This depends on the correct practice of actions to be adopted or discarded
By considering well the causality of white and black karmas.
I, a yogi, practiced in this way.
You, who seek liberation, should do likewise.

Until you obtain a fully-qualified rebirth
No breakthrough in the practice of the extraordinary path will occur.
Hence, cultivate its complete cause, missing nothing.
Especially, it is essential to purify the karmic obscurations
Of non-virtues and infractions that pollute the three doors.
Hence, cherish the cultivation of the four opponent powers constantly.
I, a yogi, practiced in this way.
You, who seek liberation, should do likewise.

If you make no effort to ponder the faults of true suffering
A genuine wish for liberation will not arise.
If you do not contemplate how the origin of suffering leads to samsara
You will not know how to eliminate the root of samsara;
Hence, it is essential to cultivate renunciation of samsara
And recognize what binds you in samsara.
I, a yogi, practiced in this way.
You, who seek liberation, should do likewise.

Bodhicitta is the trunk of the tree of the Supreme Vehicle's path
The foundation and basis of the great practices.
It is like an elixir for the Two Accumulations
It is a treasury of merit containing countless virtues.
Knowing this, the courageous Children of the Victors
Hold this precious, supreme aspiration as their core practice.
I, a yogi, practiced in this way.
You, who seek liberation, should do likewise.

Generosity is the wish-fulfilling gem that satisfies the hopes of wanderers
The superior weapon that cuts the knot of miserliness
The *bodhisattva* deed that generates unfailing courage
And the foundation of glory that roars in the ten directions.
Knowing this, the learned ones cultivate the noble path
Of giving one's body, possessions and virtues.
I, a yogi, practiced in this way.
You, who seek liberation, should do likewise.

Ethics is the water that cleanses the stains of misdeeds
The moonlight that soothes the tormenting heat of delusions.
One stands majestically like Meru amidst sentient beings
Without intimidation all beings bow down to you.
Knowing this, the worthy ones guard
Their well-accepted ethics like their eyes.

I, a yogi, practiced in this way.
You, who seek liberation, should do likewise.

Patience is the finest ornament of the Powerful Ones
The best ascetic practice for the tormenting afflictions
The garuda, the enemy of the snake of hatred
The stout armor against the weapons of harsh speech.
Knowing this, by various means
They cultivate the excellent armor of patience.
I, a yogi, practiced in this way.
You, who seek liberation, should do likewise.

If one dons the armor of unwavering joyous effort
The virtues of scriptural knowledge and insight will increase
like the waxing moon
All activities will become meaningful
Every work begun will be accomplished as desired.
Knowing this, the *bodhisattvas* practice great joyous effort
Which dispels all laziness.
I, a yogi, practiced in this way.
You, who seek liberation, should do likewise.

Meditative concentration is the king that rules the mind
When remaining focused it is immovable like
the King of Mountains
When directed it engages with all the objects
of the virtuous mind
And induces functional bliss for the body and mind.
Knowing this, the great yogis always rely upon *samadhi*
The destroyer of the enemy of mental distractions.
I, a yogi, practiced in this way.
You, who seek liberation, should do likewise.

Wisdom is the eye through which to see profound reality
The path that eliminates the root of samsara
The treasury of virtues praised in all the scriptures

Renowned as the excellent lamp that dispels the darkness
of ignorance.
Knowing this, the learned ones who seek liberation
Dedicate every effort to generate the path.
I, a yogi, practiced in this way.
You, who seek liberation, should do likewise.

Single-pointed concentration alone
Is seen as powerless to eliminate the root of samsara.
Insight devoid of the path of calm abiding
Cannot overcome the afflictions, however much it analyzes.
Hence, the insight that resolves the mode of being of things
Should mount the horse of unwavering calm abiding
And, through the sharp weapon of Madhyamika reasoning,
free from extremes
All the extreme graspings are destroyed.
With the vast insight that correctly analyzes thus
The intelligence that realizes the reality is expanded.
I, a yogi, practiced in this way.
You, who seek liberation, should do likewise.

Single-pointed familiarization evidently brings
meditative concentration
Yet the correct analysis of the mode of being of things
By the [insight of] individual investigation
Also generates meditative concentration which remains firm
and unwavering.
Seeing this, how marvelous are those who strive to accomplish
Such a union of calm abiding and special insight!
I, a yogi, practiced in this way.
You, who seek liberation, should do likewise.

Meditating on the space-like emptiness of meditative equipoise
And the illusion-like emptiness of the post-meditation state
And engaging in the practices of *bodhisattvas* –
Through the union of method and wisdom – is praiseworthy.

Understanding this, not being satisfied with the partial path
Is the tradition of the Fortunate Ones.
I, a yogi, practiced in this way.
You, who seek liberation, should do likewise.

Thus, generating the common path, which is essential for both
The Causal and Resultant Vehicles of Mahayana
And then, through a proficient captain's guidance
Entering into the ocean of *Tantras*
And receiving the complete quintessential instruction
Is the way to make human rebirth meaningful.
I, a yogi, practiced in this way.
You, who seek liberation, should do likewise.

In order to make familiar in my own mind
And also to benefit other fortunate beings
I have herein explained in an easy manner
The complete path that pleases the Victors.
I pray and dedicate any merit thus created
For all sentient beings not to be separated from
the pure and noble path.
I, a yogi, practiced in this way.
You, who seek liberation, should do likewise.

The colophon: This short presentation of the practice of the Stages on the Path to Enlightenment is written by Bhikshu Lobsang Dakpa, a hermit who has done extensive studies on dharma in order to remind himself of the practices. Composed at the Victorious Monastery of Geden, on Drok Mountain.

Prologue to The Essence of Superfine Gold

The Third Dalai Lama

I respectfully prostrate and take refuge at the feet of the venerable guru, the great being – the embodiment of the Three Jewels. Please bless me.

The spiritual system known as the Stages of the Path to Enlightenment (*Lamrim*) is what those wishing to elicit the essence of this human life of leisure and endowments should practice. It is the essence of all the teachings of the Buddha, the one and only path trodden by the Superior Beings of the three times;[1] the tradition of the [two] great refounders, Nagarjuna and Asanga; the Dharma doctrine of the excellent beings journeying towards the level of omniscience; and it covers, without omission, the steps of the paths of the beings of three capacities.[2]

1

The Authenticity and Excellence of the Lamrim

First of all, the *Lamrim* tradition – the Dharma that is to be practiced -- should have an exalted and authentic source. This Dharma, originating from genuine sources, should constitute not a partial but a thoroughly complete and unmistaken path.

The Dharma which you are going to practice today has been successively transmitted from the completely perfected Buddha to the two [refounders], Nagarjuna and Asanga; hence it has an authentic source. The stages of the path, transmitted from those authentic sources, fulfils all the wishes of beings easily and quickly; hence, it is like the king of the precious wish-fulfilling gems. As it combines the rivers of the entire excellent explanations of the sublime scriptures of Hinayana and Mahayana, it is like an ocean. As it shows in a condensed manner the core of the Sutra and Tantra, its content is complete. As it is principally aimed at taming the mind in a progressive manner, it is easy to practice. Since it is complemented with the instructions of Vidyakokila, one who was proficient in the tradition of Nagarjuna, and the instructions of Sauvarnadvipiya,[3] one who was proficient in the tradition of Asanga, you are indeed fortunate to be able to hear, contemplate and meditate upon such a teaching. Our spiritual master,[4] too, says in his *A Song of Experience*:

> The stages of the path to enlightenment
> Have been transmitted in succession through Nagarjuna and Asanga
> The crowning jewels of the learned ones of the world

Whose banner of renown rises high amongst all beings.
As it fulfills every aspiration of sentient beings
It is the king of wish-fulfilling gems of instruction
As it combines the thousand streams of noble teachings
It is also an ocean of glorious, excellent explanations.

2

The Greatness of the Instructions of the Lamrim

Thus, this instruction [on *Lamrim*] is more exalted than others with respect to four greatnesses.

1. By relying on this instruction one understands that, of the entire scriptures of the Buddha, some reveal the primary paths while others reveal the secondary paths, and one understands that they are all either directly or indirectly the prerequisites for an individual such as myself to become enlightened. Hence, this instruction has the greatness of bringing realization that the entire teaching of the Buddha is non-contradictory.

2. With this instruction, the false conceptions – that the scriptures of Sutra and Tantra, and their authoritative expositions, are merely theoretical teachings for intellectual knowledge and that there are other branches of teachings showing the essential practices which are not included in these scriptures – will be eliminated completely. Thereby, the entire subject matter of the teachings of the Buddha, and their authentic treatises – from the teachings on how to follow a spiritual master up to those on calm abiding (*shamatha*) and special insight (*vipashyana*) – is condensed in the *Lamrim* and held as the principal instruction; and since the *Lamrim* shows the instructions for the practices of analytical meditation wherever needed, and of stabilizing meditation wherever needed, one understands that it is the spiritual instruction revealing these practices. Thus, this instruction has the greatness of reflecting that all the teachings of the Buddha are spiritual advice.

3. Although all the classics, the teachings of the Buddha and their elucidations, are the most exalted spiritual advice, a beginner such as me, who has not studied such extensive teachings, cannot precisely comprehend the meanings of the scriptures. Even if I were to engage in studying and contemplating them, I would not understand the true meanings of the classics. Even if I were to comprehend the meanings, it would take a tremendous effort and a long time for me to do so. Thus, by relying on [an instruction] such as the *Stages on the Path to Enlightenment*,[5] which is the quintessential instruction of the Excellent Master's *Lamp for the Path to Enlightenmen*t,[6] one discovers the meanings of the great classics without difficulty. Hence, this instruction has the greatness of easily grasping the true intent of the Buddha.

4. When one discovers these greatnesses, one understands that all the words of the Buddha, either directly or indirectly, show the methods for attaining Buddhahood. Therefore, if one holds that some [teachings of the Buddha] show the methods for Buddhahood – and therefore should be practiced – whereas others are hindrances and therefore should be abandoned, then one is actually forsaking the Dharma. By relying on this instruction, as mentioned earlier, just by ascertaining that all the teachings of the Buddha are non-contradictory the heinous negative action of forsaking the Dharma ceases by itself. Thus, this instruction has the greatness of preventing the grave misdeed of forsaking the Dharma.

Thus, for those who have the intelligence, or those who aspire to have the intelligence, to examine the meaning of the scriptures, it is appropriate for those who are helplessly enchanted by this instruction to engage in listening, contemplation and meditation on this excellent instruction – the Stages of the Path of the Beings of Three Capacities , which has been relied upon and practiced by many fortunate and learned ones of India and Tibet – because it has the four greatnesses mentioned above. The Venerable Master also says:

It makes one realize that the entire teaching is consistent
It makes one see the entire teaching as spiritual instruction
It makes one discover the intent of the Buddha with ease
And it also saves one from the abyss of grave misdeeds.
Hence, which intelligent being would not be enthralled
By the Stages of the Path of the Beings of Three Capacities
The excellent instruction relied upon by the many fortunate beings
The learned ones of India and Tibet?

3

How to Listen to and Explain the Teachings

The Benefits of Listening to and Explaining the Teaching

With respect to this instruction, possessing the four greatnesses unifying the essence of all the scriptures of the Buddha, one should consider the benefits of teaching and explaining correctly even a part of it, let alone the entire stages of the path of the beings of three capacities. By developing reverence for the Teacher (the Buddha) and Dharma, if one correctly teaches it to suitable vessels with pure motivation and conduct then it is certain that great benefit will accrue from explaining the sacred Dharma. And if one correctly listens to it by abandoning the three faults of a vessel,[7] and applying the six attitudes,[8] then it is also certain that great benefit will accrue from listening to the sacred Dharma. Therefore, it is logical to strive to explain and listen to the instruction correctly because the Venerable Master says:

> As the essence of the entire scripture is herein condensed
> Even listening to or explaining this teaching once
> Certainly accumulates a great virtue of teaching or listening
> To the holy Dharma; hence, contemplate this.

The Qualifications of the Spiritual Teacher

If there are such great benefits from listening to this instruction correctly, then from what kind of person should one hear this extraordinary instruction? In general, with respect to teachers worthy of listening to the sacred teachings, various qualifications are set down in the context of Hinayana, Mahayana, Sutra and Tantra teachings. However, the kind of spiritual teacher from whom one receives a precious instruction such as this should have the qualities mentioned in [Maitreya's] *Ornament of Mahayana Sutras.*

He should possess the qualities of spiritual realization that subdue his mind-stream through the Three Higher Trainings: He should be (i) disciplined through the higher training of morality, (ii) calmed through the higher training of meditative concentration, and (iii) thoroughly pacified through the higher training of insight. (iv) He should have qualities of abundant learning from the Three Scriptural Collections[9] and so forth. (v) He should possess the insight that thoroughly realizes reality (emptiness). (vi) He should possess more good qualities than his disciples. These are the six qualities developed personally by the spiritual teacher.

Then (i) he should be skilled in the methods of leading [the disciples] on the stages of the path and be sufficiently eloquent to touch their hearts. (ii) He should possess pure motivation of love [towards the disciples] and teach the disciples out of compassion without looking for wealth, fame and so forth. (iii) He should possess joyous effort in teaching and so forth for the welfare of others. (iv) He should endure hardships in teaching and should not lose patience over the wrong practices of his disciples. These are the four altruistic qualities [of the teacher] in taking care of others.

Thus, by seeking a spiritual teacher with these ten qualifications, you should receive instructions and teachings on Mahayana.

The Qualifications of the Disciple

In general, a disciple who listens to the teachings should (i) be impartial, (ii) have the intelligence to distinguish between the correct and incorrect paths, and (iii) be interested in pursuing the correct path. On top of these three, (iv) he should have respect for the teaching and the teacher.

In particular, a qualified disciple who is suitable to be led along a path such as this should possess these four qualifications: He should (i) have a great interest in the Dharma, (ii) be attentive while listening to the Dharma, (iii) have great faith in and respect for the Dharma and the teacher and, (iv) reject faulty explanations and retain good explanations. (v) As a conducive condition for the fourth qualification he should have discrimination, and (vi) to eliminate unfavorable conditions he should be without prejudice. Thus, one should possess these six qualifications [to listen to this teaching].

Therefore, if you wish to become a qualified teacher of this path you should strive to acquire the above qualities of a spiritual teacher. When listening to the teaching on this path you should train yourself to cultivate the qualifications of a disciple.

4

How to Rely on the Spiritual Teacher

Preliminary Practice

This is how to practice the path of the three types of beings after having heard the instructions on them from a qualified spiritual teacher: First, arrange representations of the [Three] Jewels in a favorable and pleasant place. Arrange offerings without deceit [or without untidiness]. Sit cross-legged on a comfortable seat. From the depths of your heart entrust yourself [to the Three Jewels] and within your mind assimilate the practice of taking refuge as much as possible. Meditate on the Four Immeasurables.[10] Generate the mind of enlightenment (*bodhicitta*) by reciting the lines: "To Buddha, Dharma and Sangha..."

With [the recitation of] "*Om svabhava...*" all phenomena become empty, empty of inherent existence. From within emptiness, in the space in front, upon a large and spacious jeweled throne supported by eight snow lions are cushions of the variegated lotus and a moon disc. Upon this is seated our Teacher (the Buddha) – who is inseparable from your spiritual master – showing you this path. He is surrounded by the lineage masters of the extensive path of conduct and the profound path of view. Around them are oceans of the Buddhas of the ten directions, Bodhisattvas, Hearers, Solitary Realizers, Viras, Dakinis and Dharma Protectors. Invite them by reciting:

> Without wavering from the perfect reality of phenomena
> Compassionately looking at the limitless sentient beings
>   of the ten directions

O Gurus of the three times and your entourage
Who spread the benevolent deeds of the entire Buddhas,
please grace us with your presence.

Protector of all sentient beings without exception...

Practice the following as given in [Shantideva's] *Guide to the Bodhisattva's Way of Life*: While reciting the lines, "To this very fragrant bathing chamber ..." visualize a bathing chamber, bathe, dry, offer clothes and ornaments [to them]. While reciting, "Out of compassion, for me and sentient beings ..." make ritual offerings to them and request them to remain as our field of merit.

Then do the seven-limbed practice, which is comprised of the essential practices of accumulation [of merit] and purification [of negativities], as follows. First of all recite the lines, "You are the embodiment of all the Buddhas ..." Then recite the lines, "The realizers of truth, Tilopa and ..." for the lineage masters of the experiential path of blessing. Then recite the lines, "Maitreya, Asanga, Vasubhandu, Vimuktisena ..." for the lineage masters of the extensive path of conduct. Then recite the lines, "To Manjushri, Nagarjuna, the destroyer of grasping at 'is' and 'is not' ..." for the lineage masters of the profound of view. Then recite the lines, "In front of the Buddha ..." for the Lord [Atisha]. Then recite the lines, "To the spiritual master of the entire ..." for Drom [Tonpa]. Then recite the lines, "Avalokiteshvara, the great treasure of non-objectifying compassion ..." for the Venerable [Tsongkhapa]. Then recite the lines, "Gaining strength of the powerful and profound insight ..." Then recite the lines, "To those with excellent awareness and liberation ..." Then recite the lines, "The source of all fulfillments ..." Then recite the lines, "To those who trained us in the sciences ..." Then recite the lines, "To the precious Buddha, a peerless teacher ..." Then recite the lines, "Through skilful means and compassion you took birth in the Shakya family ..." Then recite the lines beginning with. "To as many of you as ..." through to "... I prostrate and make offerings."

Following this recite either the long or short version of the mandala offering. Then recite the lines beginning with, "Offerings other than these ..." through to "May these clouds of offerings remain distinct." Then recite the *General Confession* three times. Then recite the lines beginning with, "Overpowered by attachment, hatred, and ignorance ..." through to "... dedicate to the Buddhahood."

Now chant the *Opening of the Door of the Supreme Path* – a supplication to the lineage of masters of the *Lamrim* – in a devout tone. Then say, "May the recipients of these offerings return to their natural abodes" and request them to depart.

If you engage in this [preliminary practice] either four or six times a day, then perform the departure at the final session. These are the preliminaries to the practice of relying on a spiritual master.

The Actual Method of Relying Upon the Spiritual Teacher

The real practice of relying on a spiritual teacher is through analytical meditation. So, think like this: My glorious spiritual teachers are the root of all spiritual attainments and the source of all goodness in this and future lives. Just like a doctor to a patient, the teachers are kind to me as they cure my disease of suffering. I have been wandering in the cycle of existence forever until now, since time without beginning, because either I have not met spiritual teachers or, even if I may have met them, I did not follow their words correctly. Now I must please my spiritual teachers in whatever way possible. It would be more kind to give a bowl of food to someone on the verge of starving to death than to give someone as much gold as his hands can carry when that person is replete with food and wealth. Likewise, for me the kindness of my spiritual teachers is certainly greater than that of the Buddhas, just as is stated in [Nagarjuna's] *Five Stages*:

> He is the self-born Bhagavan
> The only exalted deity.

As he perfectly bestows the core instructions
The *vajra* master surpasses Him.

In his past lives our Teacher (the Buddha) offered one-hundred-thousand gold coins in order to repay the kindness of one of his spiritual teachers from whom he had heard half a verse: "If there is birth, there is death. Cessation of this is blissful". He also offered up his closest ones such as his prince and queen, and even offered a thousand butter lamps burning on his body in order to repay the kindness of – or to please – his teachers from whom he heard a verse. In these, and other ways, the Buddha offered his body and all that he possessed. Since I am a follower of this Buddha, and I too have heard unlimited teachings from my present spiritual teachers, how immeasurable their kindness is to me!

There are people who only feel grateful if their teachers are more erudite than they are. Otherwise, without any reverence, they boastfully say, "I have already heard your teachings!" This is a great mistake. For instance, even if your parents are not learned, you should still be grateful for their kindness as there is great benefit in doing so and great disadvantage in not doing so. Likewise, this is true with regard to your spiritual teachers.

If you acknowledge that even someone who now gives you a little wealth is kind, then your spiritual teachers are all those who bring you happiness in this and futures lives. If you examine this carefully, it is obvious that the difference in the degree of happiness and suffering experienced by all, from the elevated ones – the Buddhas and Bodhisattvas – down to the ordinary householders, depends entirely upon how they have pleased or displeased the spiritual teachers. Moreover, there were many who were led to Buddhahood by their spiritual teachers in one lifetime.

If I also please my spiritual teachers with the three-fold offering,[11] I can certainly attain Buddhahood. Since the kindness of my spiritual teachers is inconceivable, it is of utmost importance to please my gurus because even meeting noble teachers and being guided by them in future lives solely depends upon pleasing the present teachers with whom I have a spiritual connection. Thus, there is no way other than avoiding the wrong ways of relying upon your spiritual teachers.

It is repeatedly said in all *sutra*s and their treatises, "Please your spiritual guides!" This is not an unwanted injuction or a burden put upon me. There is nobody who does not want virtuous merit. All *sutras*, *tantras* and their treatises mention that there is no greater field for gathering virtuous merit than through ones' spiritual teachers.

When you undertatake to please your spiritual masters, from the very beginning do not let any negative thoughts about them cross your mind. By perceiving whatever they do as excellent deeds, cultivate faith in them from the depths of your heart, not just in words alone. Do this until the mere utterance of their names, or a thought of them, makes the hairs on your body tingle or until you are in tears or whatever.

In general, since the Buddhas and Bodhisattvas have said that you should not dwell on the faults of other sentient beings, what need is there to mention faults with regard to your spiritual teachers? Even if they appear to have faults, this is only your impure perception. How can a spiritual teacher have such faults?

Once, after having meditated on Maitreya, Arya Asanga saw a bitch whose lower torso was full of maggots. Naropa saw Tilopa roasting fish alive, and so forth.[12] And in *sutras* such as *A Meeting of the Father and Son* it is said that the Buddhas may even manifest as demons in order to help sentient beings. Thus, how can you think of spiritual teachers having faults? Contemplate that they definitely are real Buddhas!

On the contrary, if you belittle and despise your spiritual teachers with distorted thoughts about them, then this is said to be the gravest unwholesome deed of all negative actions in the *Guhyasamaja Root Tantra*, [Ashvagosha's] *Fifty Verses on the Guru* and so forth. Thus, taking the life story of Drom Tonpa as an example, I shall not seek out many spiritual teachers in haste. Whoever I accept as my spiritual teacher, I shall never ever let disrespectful thoughts about him cross my mind, even at the cost of my life. The Venerable Master also has instructed with immense love:

> To fulfill all ideal conditions for the good of this and future lives
> The root lies in our spiritual masters, the guides on our path.
> Seeing this, follow them properly in thought and deed
> Forsaking them not even at the cost of your life
> And please them with the offering of practice – heeding their words.
> I, a yogi, practiced in this way.
> You, who seek liberation, should do likewise.

5

Training the Mind after Reliance upon the Spiritual Teacher

Contemplating the Great Importance of the Life of Leisure and Endowments

So, if the way to persevere, relying upon and pleasing the spiritual teachers who show you the path, is through the offering of practice in accordance with their instructions, then what kind of instructions should you follow? There is no greater offering of the practice of following the instructions of the teachers than making this human life of leisure and endowments – which is extremely difficult to obtain with respect to its causes and effects, but which, once found, can be of immense purpose and be greater than a wish-fulfilling jewel – a meaningful one by correctly practicing the sacred Dharma as instructed by the teachers. Therefore, grit your teeth and think, if I do not prevent this human life – found just this once – from slipping away worthlessly then I must be weak-hearted.

If I do not forcefully give up the eight varieties of worldly concerns – winning out over my adversaries and promoting my relatives in this life to impress others, teaching and hearing Dharma or keeping vows and so forth while motivated by the thought of gaining wealth and honor – and practice a Dharma such as meditation on impermanence both in words and deeds, more than anything I will run the risk of forfeiting my future. In this life, if I practice the pure Dharma so as not to let myself down, then a stable foundation for my everlasting ultimate goal will be established, and this is better than anything else. Therefore, I should turn away from meaningless worldly activities – which are both less beneficial and more hazardous – like winnowing the husks from grain, and I should make this human life a meaningful and purposeful one so that I may not have regrets at the time of death. Moreover, I should generate the wish to extract the essence of this human life right away, just as a thirsty person searches for water. Reflect that the Venerable Master also says thus:

> This opportune life surpasses a wish-fulfilling gem
> Such is found only once this time
> So hard to obtain yet so easy to lose like a flash of lightning!
> Seeing this nature, discard all worldly activities
> Just like winnowing the chaff
> And, day and night, make it meaningful.

6

How to Extract the Essence of this Life of Leisure and Endowment

If you are to elicit the essence of this human life of leisure and endowment, then how should you do this? This is explained under two headings; how to generate conviction in the general presentation of the path and the actual way to extract the essence.

How to Generate Conviction in the General Presentation of the Path

It is extremely important to have an understanding of how to generate conviction in the general presentation of the paths. Therefore, I will explain briefly, under two headings, how the paths of the beings of three capacities encompass the entire teaching and the reasons for guiding [practitioners] through the paths of the beings of three capacities.

1. How the Paths of the Beings of Three Capacities Encompass the Entire Teaching

In the beginning the Buddha generated *bodhicitta*, in the middle he amassed the accumulations [of merit and wisdom] and finally he became a Buddha. He did all of this for the benefit of sentient beings. The teachings he gave are also solely to help sentient beings. Regarding this objective, there are two benefits for sentient beings – the temporary and the ultimate, which are higher rebirth and definite goodness respectively. Of these two, all teachings that are given to accomplish the former come under the cycle of teachings meant for beings of lesser capacity or practices shared with them. The characteristics of beings of lesser capacity are outlined in *A Lamp on the Path to Enlightenment*:

> Whoever, by whatever means
> Aims merely for happiness in *samsara*[13]
> And pursues it for himself
> Is understood to be a being of the lowest capacity.

As is said here, a being of low capacity does not concern himself much with this life, but pursues the happiness of higher rebirths in future lives and practices the causes leading to it.

The ultimate benefit of definite goodness is twofold – mere liberation from cyclic existence and omniscience. All the teachings given to accomplish the former come under the cycle meant for beings of medium capacity or practices shared with them. It is stated in *A Lamp on the Path to Enlightenment*:

> One who turns his back on the delights of *samsara*
> Averting negative actions
> Aiming at mere peace, solely for himself
> Is known as a being of medium capacity.

Thus, a being of average capacity turns his back on the highest achievements of *samsara* and sets the goal of accomplishing mere liberation from *samsara* for himself, and to do so engages in the practice of the Three Higher Trainings.

The means of attaining the exalted state of omniscience are the Mantra and Perfection Vehicles, both of which come under the cycle of teachings for a being of great capacity. *A Lamp on the Path to Enlightenment* says:

> One who, seeing the suffering within himself
> Wishes to extinguish the sufferings
> Of others completely –
> That being is the most excellent one.

As is stated here, a being of great capacity is one who, overpowered by compassion, aims to attain the state of omniscience through training in the Six Perfections and the Two Stages in order to extinguish all the sufferings of other sentient beings.

2. The Reasons for Guiding Practitioners Through the Paths of the Three Types of Beings

Although the practices of the beings of three capacities are taught here, in this context one should be able take the practices pertaining to the two lower categories of beings as branches leading to the path of a being of great capacity. Here the practitioner is not instructed to follow the mere path of a being of lesser capacity, who merely aims for the highest achievements of *samsara*, nor is he instructed to follow the mere path of a being of medium capacity who merely aims to achieve liberation from *samsara*. But, in fact, some paths shared with these two types of beings are preliminaries leading to the path of a being of great capacity.

The reason behind this is that there is no gateway to enter into Mahayana other than generating the supreme *bodhicitta*, and hence it is necessary to generate *bodhicitta*. As a prelude to this, one must develop the power of enthusiasm for *bodhicitta* by contemplating the benefits thereof. As for the benefits of *bodhicitta*, in short there are two; the temporary and the ultimate. The temporary fruits of the happiness of higher rebirth can easily be accomplished through *bodhicitta*. The ultimate state of omniscience also results from *bodhicitta*. Therefore, one must generate *bodhicitta*.

This in turn must be preceded by great compassion; an empathy that cannot bear the sufferings tormenting all sentient beings. For this it is essential to have a strong sense of aversion for the suffering that torments oneself. Thus, initially, within the context of the path of a being of lesser capacity, contemplate how one is tormented by the sufferings of the lower realms and generate a wish to be freed from them. And within the context of the path of a being of medium capacity, contemplate that even in the higher realms of existence there is no true happiness and generate renunciation from the whole of *samsara*. After that, based on your own experience, you should cultivate love, compassion and *bodhicitta* wishing to free all mother sentient beings who are tormented by suffering. Hence, training in the shared paths of the beings of the lesser and medium capacities is the best means of guiding a practitioner to the path of a great being.

The Actual Way to Extract the Essence

There are three actual ways of drawing out the essence [of human life]; training in the path shared with beings of lesser capacity, training in the path shared with beings of medium capacity and training in the path of beings of great capacity. These ways of training are explained in the following chapters.

7

Training in the Path Shared with Beings of Lesser Capacity

Mindfulness of Death

Contemplate this with full concentration: Although I have found this precious human life, which is difficult to come by – but, once found, meaningful – it will not last long. Death is inevitable. Yet, there is no certainty of when I am going to die. Hence, I must work hard to make the most of this life now. So far, people from all classes of society – high, middle and low – have been swiftly overcome by the Lord of Death, like the crowds in a bustling market place. How fortunate I am to have stayed alive thus far! Feel the heart-wrenching sensation. Generate such awareness of death that you cannot bear to stay in one place any longer. Contemplate that when you die you will have no choice but to go alone without the company of your near and dear ones and your wealth and possessions. Instead, you will have to carry over all of the unwholesome actions you have accumulated for their sake. All the enjoyments of this life, good food and drink, people and wealth, have [so far] disappeared into thin air. So now think "I will genuinely practice the Dharma for whatever lifespan I have left". And also that "I must start from today itself".

Contemplation that at the Time of Death Nothing Helps Except Dharma

At the time of death, if nothing can help me except the Dharma, then how will the Dharma help me and non-Dharma harm me? Even after death I will not turn into nothing, but will certainly be reborn. As for rebirth, I will either be reborn in the fortunate or unfortunate realms of existence, and nowhere else. That too is determined by my actions over which I will have no control. I will have to take rebirth propelled by my positive or negative actions. If wholesome thoughts arise in me at the time of dying, then I will be born into the fortunate realms of existence. Whereas if unwholesome thoughts arise at that time, then I will be born into one of the three unfortunate realms and suffer intensely.

Reflecting on Sufferings of the Lower Realms

What are the kinds of suffering in the unfortunate realms? Lord Nagarjuna says:

> Each day recall the intense
> Hot and cold hell realms.
> Remember also the hungry ghosts
> Who are emaciated by hunger and thirst.
> See and reflect on the animals
> Who are full of the suffering of stupidity.
> Abandon the causes of these and cultivate
> the causes of fortunate realms.
> Having obtained the hard-won human life
> On this Earth, be alert to sever
> The causes of unfortunate rebirths.

As said above, there are unbearable sufferings of heat and cold in the hell realms. The hungry ghosts experience unendurable sufferings of hunger and thirst, and the animals, unbearable sufferings of preying upon one another, stupidity and foolishness and so forth. At present, I cannot tolerate holding out my hand in a blazing fire even for a moment. I cannot tolerate staying naked even for a day in the bitter cold of winter. I cannot tolerate staying hungry for several days on end. I cannot even tolerate the sting of a bee and so on. How then could I tolerate the sufferings of the hot and cold hell realms, the suffering of hunger and thirst of the hungry ghost realm, and the sufferings of devouring each other alive, and so forth, of the animal realm? So, based on your own experience, now meditate on the torments of the lower realms until the fear and terror of the sufferings of these realms overwhelms your mind.

Thus, contemplate: "Having found this excellent life of a human being, now I shall strive to avoid rebirth in the unfortunate realms by discarding their causes and cultivating the causes of the fortunate realms."

Training in the Practice of Refuge, the Sacred Gateway to Buddhism

How should one strive to avert birth in the unfortunate realms? As explained above, one should fear the sufferings of the lower realms and think that the Three Jewels have the power to protect you from them. Knowing this, take refuge in the Three Jewels from the depths of your heart. Indeed, the Three Jewels can protect you from the fears of the unfortunate realms because the Buddha Jewel is himself free from all fears, is skilled in the methods of freeing others from all fears, engages in great compassion towards all sentient beings impartially and works for all – no matter whether they have benefited him or not. Hence, he is a worthy object of refuge. This also holds true for the Dharma Jewel and *Sangha* Jewel.

The teachers, doctrines and spiritual communities of the non-Buddhist schools do not have any of these qualities. Hence, they are not worthy objects of refuge. Since the Three Jewels have these qualities they are worthy objects of refuge.

How should you seek refuge? You should sincerely go for refuge in the Three Jewels by entrusting yourself to them completely while chanting:

> I go for refuge to the Buddha, the supreme one amongst bipeds;
> Please be my teacher to free me from the sufferings of *samsara* and the unfortunate realms.
> I go for refuge to the Dharma, the supreme one amongst all those free from desire;
> Please be my actual refuge to free me from the sufferings of *samsara* and the lower realms.
> I go for refuge to the Sangha, the supreme amongst all communities;
> Please be my spiritual companion to free me from the sufferings of *samsara* and the unfortunate realms.

Thus having sought refuge in the Three Jewels, if you do not follow the precepts of refuge you will degenerate in terms of the refuge practices. Hence, train yourself in the precepts of refuge.

In fact, once you have taken refuge in the Buddha, you should no longer regard the fierce worldly gods such as Vishnu and others as objects of refuge. But you should perceive all images of Buddhas as real Buddhas and respect them.

Once you have taken refuge in the Dharma you should cease to harm sentient beings. You should never disrespect even a single letter [of the scriptures] and show them respect.

Once you have taken refuge in the Sangha you should not associate and become intimate with heretics (*tirthikas*) and evil friends. You should never disrespect anyone wearing saffron robes but show respect to them.

Moreover, knowing that every happiness and welfare, virtue and goodness is a result of the kindness of the Three Jewels, offer to the Three Jewels the first serving of food or drink and so forth. You should approach your short-term and long-term goals by praying to the Three Jewels and not by relying upon the ordinary *mo* diviners, Bon priests and so forth.

You should bring others into the fold of refuge in the Three Jewels to the best of your ability. Think three times a day and three times each night that you will not forsake the Three Jewels, even at the cost of your life, and that you will not even let a single word that denies them slip from your tongue. Seek refuge in the Three Jewels from the depths of your heart three times a day and three times each night through understanding their virtues and distinctive characteristics, understanding your commitments, and without taking others as objects of refuge.

Developing Conviction in the Law of Causality

Although by going for refuge to the Three Jewels you will be protected from the sufferings of the unfortunate realms, what causes should be cultivated in order to achieve rebirth in the higher realms? By reflecting on the causes and effects of virtuous and non-virtuous actions, contemplate how every virtuous and non-virtuous action is individually certain, every virtuous and non-virtuous action multiplies greatly, actions not taken will not produce a result and action taken will not go to waste. You should cultivate virtuous actions and discard non-virtuous actions accordingly.

We cannot prove the law of karma through the power of factual reasoning. It says in the *Sutra of the King of Concentration*:

> Moon and stars may fall
> Mountains and valleys may crumble
> And space may change its appearance
> But, you never speak false words.

So, by feeling totally convinced of the words of the Buddha, you should avoid all negative actions in general, and in particular you should consider that the karma of committing the ten non-virtuous actions through the three doors [body, speech and mind], heavy, medium and small, will ripen as rebirth in the lower realms or will produce unpleasant effects [in terms of the five kinds of karmic fruition] such as fruition corresponding with their cause and environmental determination as stated in the following verses [of Shantideva's *A Guide to the Bodhisattva's Way of Life*]:

From unwholesome actions come sufferings
Thus, day and night
It is worthwhile for me to contemplate merely
On how I should free myself from these.

And,

Faith is the root of all types of virtues
As said by the Buddha.
The root of faith lies
In constant reflection on the ripening effects.

The *Truth Speaker's Chapter* says:

O King, do not commit killing!
Life is dear to all beings.
Thus, whoever wishes longevity
Must not have even an inkling to kill.

As stated here, you should repeatedly resolve to refrain from all negative actions such as killing – not letting even the thought of such actions cross your mind – and cultivate all the wholesome actions of not killing and so forth. The Venerable Master also says:

You are unsure about your birth in the unfortunate realms
after death
And certain that the Three Jewels are the protectors from this terror.
So, make your practice of refuge firm
And let not the precepts of your refuge degenerate.
This depends on the correct practice of actions to be adopted
or discarded
By considering well the causality of white and black karmas.

By observing the ethics of abandoning the ten unwholesome actions, one obtains a good rebirth. However, in order to accomplish the sublime path to omniscience one must obtain a rebirth attributed to the eight matured karmas such as [birth in] a noble family lineage and having a beautiful body. Therefore, one should be mindful of practicing the cultivation of their causes, such as giving up harming sentient beings, offering butter lamps, new clothes and so forth, and respecting others by overcoming arrogance.

However, if due to excessive mental afflictions, and so forth, you are defiled by non-virtues and infractions, you should not show indifference towards them. Instead, restore the infractions accordingly and confess the non-virtuous actions by applying all of the four powerful antidotes. And continuously make the effort not to defile your body, speech and mind with non-virtues and infractions as the Venerable Master also advises:

> Until you obtain a fully-qualified rebirth
> No breakthrough in the practice of the extraordinary path
> will occur.
> Hence, cultivate its complete cause, missing nothing.
> Especially, it is essential to purify the karmic obscurations
> Of non-virtues and infractions that pollute the three doors.
> Hence, cherish the cultivation of the four opponent powers
> constantly.

By meditating in this way, whenever you generate a genuine interest in pursuing the excellence of future lives by feeling revulsion towards this life, then you have succeeded in the training on the path of a being of lesser capacity.

8

Training in the Path Shared with Beings of Medium Capacity

Although by abandoning the ten unwholesome actions, and cultivating the ten wholesome actions, you may achieve an extraordinary rebirth in a higher realm, you have still not transcended the sufferings of *samsara*. Hence, you should attain *moksha* – the liberation totally beyond all suffering.

Contemplating the Sufferings of Samsara

Why is the whole of *samsara* suffering by its very nature? The three unfortunate realms were explained earlier. However, in the present context you should take a slightly different approach which is to consider the sufferings of those unfortunate realms individually. Following this you should reflect, "I cannot tolerate such intense and lasting suffering. Therefore, at any cost, I must attain liberation, the abandonment of all the sufferings of *samsara*, including those [sufferings of the unfortunate realms]."

None of the high or low *samsaric* existences other than the unfortunate realms are also not beyond suffering by nature. In the case of humans, while in the mother's womb, from conception, we suffer from darkness, bad smells, much filth and so forth. In the thirty-eighth week, at delivery, driven by the force of the wind of previous karma, we suffer painfully as if being pulled through the hole of a vice or being crushed like a sesame seed. After birth, even when laid on very soft bedding we suffer as if we have fallen into a bed of thorns. Such are the sufferings of birth.

After birth, the youthful body eventually bends like a bow, hair turns gray like *tawa* flowers[14] and the forehead fills with wrinkles like strips of shredded leather; while sitting, we drop like a load breaking free of its rope, and while getting up we are like a tree being uprooted. We stammer in our speech and stagger in our walk. Our eyes, ears and so forth cannot perceive objects clearly. Our body pales, resembling a corpse. We become forgetful as memory fades. We have difficulty digesting our meals and cannot enjoy them as we would like. As most of our lifespan has evaporated we are fast approaching death. Such are the sufferings of old age.

When we become sick, due to an imbalance in the elements of our body, our skin dries and our flesh sags. We have to avoid desirable food and drinks, fearing that they might affect our ailments. Instead, we have to take food, drinks, medicines and so forth that we do not like. We have to undergo harsh treatments such as bloodletting and moxabustion. We experience immense suffering, fearing our ailments might not be cured. Such are the sufferings of sickness.

When stricken with a fatal disease we realize that death is inevitable. We repent our past unwholesome actions. We know this human life has been wasted on us. We are aware of separation from our body, possessions, family, friends, attendants and servants. Our mouth dries, lips remain agape, nose deflates, eyes sink in and breath comes in gasps. We are terrorized by the intense sufferings of the unfortunate realms. These are the sufferings of dying in spite of our reluctance to die.

Sometimes we meet with unwanted adversaries such as bandits and thieves who rob all our food and wealth; they strike our body with weapons, clubs and so on. At times we are tortured with various punishments at the hands of kings and so forth. Or we suffer by hearing dreadful news. Such are the sufferings of meeting with unpleasant experiences.

There is the suffering of unwillingly separating from all the wealth and possessions that you have obtained by disregarding all hardships, personal happiness and spiteful rumors, and reluctantly separating from desired objects such as those close to your heart.

With regard to the sufferings of not getting what one wants despite looking for it, they are; in the case of lay people, for example, not achieving the desired harvest – in spite of toiling on their farmland – due to drought, frost, hail and so forth; for those sailing ships, storms bringing disaster. If you are a merchant, you either lose your goods or don't make a profit, and so on. Monks and nuns suffer from their inability to observe the vows they have taken. So, these are sufferings of not attaining what you wish.

No sooner than we have taken on this appropriated aggregate [of form, i.e. body], it serves as the basis for the sufferings of sickness, ageing, dying, and so forth in this life; it induces the sufferings of our future lives; and it becomes the vessel for both the suffering of suffering and the suffering of change. Being implicated by nature in the pervasive suffering of conditioned existence, its nature is suffering and not at all that of happiness.

In the case of demi-gods, they are confined by the atrocious sufferings of having their bodies maimed and wounded. As for the gods of the desire realm, when the five signs of death befall them they suffer far more than those in the hell realms. They have unfathomable sufferings of depression, expulsion from their abode and so forth. The ordinary gods of the upper realms [of form and formlessness] do not have the suffering of suffering. However, the first three Concentrations within the form realm have the suffering of change and the Fourth Concentration and the formless realms have unendurable pervasive suffering of conditioned existence like having an intensely painful boil. This being so, we must try by all means to attain the level of liberation from all the universal and individual sufferings of *samsara*.

How to Train in Morality

In fact, liberation cannot be attained without causes and conditions. Thus, you should correctly practice the Three Higher Trainings which are the methods of attaining liberation. In other words, you should practice the higher training of morality, which is the indispensable foundation of the other two trainings. In this regard, you should check carefully – with mindfulness and vigilance – for all the causes of infraction such as ignorance, to prevent infractions from occurring in the first place. Should they occur, you should confess and resolve to refrain from it properly without harboring it for long. Thus, make the effort to cultivate the antidotes to the grosser delusions first, so that you are not sullied by moral downfalls. In whatever you do, so as not to embarrass yourself you should not go against the teachings of the Buddha. The Venerable Master also says:

> If you make no effort to ponder the faults of true suffering
> A genuine wish for liberation will not arise.
> If you do not contemplate how the origin of suffering leads
> to samsara
> You will not know how to eliminate the root of samsara;
> Hence, it is essential to cultivate renunciation of samsara
> And recognize what binds you in samsara.

Once you generate renunciation, the concept of turning away from samsara – just as a man caught in a blazing house wishes to escape from it – you have succeeded in the training in the path of a being of medium capacity.

9

Training in the Path of a Being of Great Capacity

Although you may attain mere liberation through the practice of the path, the Three Higher Trainings, it is not sufficient because once you have attained liberation – although you may not have to wander in *samsara* – you will not have attained the final goal for yourself as you will have only partially overcome the faults and partially attained the virtuous qualities. As a consequence, you cannot entirely fulfill the needs of others. Therefore, you should aim to achieve the state of Buddhahood, the fulfillment of the two goals.

Bodhicitta – Gateway to the Mahayana

Buddhahood should not be pursued for your benefit alone but for the benefit of all sentient beings. This is because, just as you have fallen into the ocean of suffering, all sentient beings are in a pathetic situation since they are also tormented by suffering. And there is not a single sentient being who has not been your parent, not only once but countless times. They are all kind to you since they have lovingly cared for you. Hence, you should generate *bodhicitta* in order to free these compassionate sentient beings from suffering and lead them to the highest state of non-abiding *nirvana.*

How to Generate Bodhicitta through the Sevenfold Cause-and-Effect Instruction

You should generate *bodhicitta* through the sevenfold cause-and-effect instruction. With regard to this instruction, the recognition of all sentient beings having been your mother gives rise to remembering their kindness. From this comes a sense of wishing to repay their kindness. From this arises the sense of attraction towards them. From this comes love and compassion that induces a courageous resolution. From this arises the genuine courageous resolution and from it comes *bodhicitta*. This is the group of seven practices from which omniscience arises.

Prior to these, you should cultivate equanimity; a sense of regarding all sentient beings equally. This is because if you have biased feelings of closeness, distance or indifference towards sentient beings, then you cannot generate a true awareness of all sentient beings as your mother. Even the little love and compassion you have generated will be somewhat prejudiced. Therefore, first, cultivate equanimity.

The method of doing this is as follows: First, observe many neutral sentient beings who have neither benefited nor harmed you in this life. Then contemplate that from their side they are equal in wanting happiness and not wanting suffering, and think that as far as I am concerned, since they have all quite simply been my parents I should not divide them into two categories, holding some to be dear and benefiting them and holding others as distant and hurting them. Instead, I shall regard them equally. Then, think of your close family members in this life equally and do the same for those who have hurt you in this life. Then, generate equanimity with regard to all sentient beings.

As there is no beginning to *samsara*, neither is there a beginning to my birth in it. Therefore, there is no place [in *samsara*] I can claim not to have taken birth. Nor is there any sentient being I can claim not to have been my mother; in fact, they have all been my mothers countless times. You do not recognize this because you have been going through the rounds of birth and death, but there is not a single sentient being who has not been your parent. Each time they were your parents they nurtured you with affection, just like your parents of this life. Hence, they are absolutely kind.

How did your mother in this life nurture you with kindness? When you were in her womb, fearing you might be harmed she took care of you by protecting you, tending to you and so on. After birth she placed you on soft fabrics, took you in her arms, gazed at you with loving eyes, smiled at you affectionately, breastfed you with love and held you close to her warm body. She fed you with her tongue, wiped off your snot with her mouth, and wiped your bottom with her hands. When you felt even slightly sick she regarded it as worse than her own life being at stake. She gave you all the wealth and possessions she had accumulated, disregarding all her hardship, happiness and suffering, feeling it too extravagant to use them for herself. In short, she protected you from harm and benefited you to the best of her ability. Reflect on this and intensely feel her kindness in your heart.

Then observe the near and dear ones related to your parents of this life and think that they have been your mothers countless times, specifically your mothers as human beings. And every time they were your mothers they protected you from harm and immensely benefited you, just like the mother of this life. Hence, they are kind. Then do the same with respect to beings you feel indifferent to and those who have hurt you in this life.

These mother sentient beings – who have nurtured you with kindness countless times – are insane and unable to control their minds due to disturbances from the demons of mental afflictions. They lack the eyes to see the paths of higher rebirth and absolute goodness because, due to their ignorance, they are blind to the sight of wisdom. They do not have spiritual teachers, the guides for the blind, to lead them to the city of liberation. Each moment, being involuntarily distracted by negative behavior, they stagger toward the fearful precipice of *samsara* and the unfortunate realms. Think, therefore, who should these poor [mother sentient beings] put their hope in, if not me? Who does the responsibility of freeing these mothers fall upon, if not me? Nothing could be a more shameful and embarrassing act than ignoring these kind mothers and selfishly working only to free yourself from *samsara*! Even though these mothers attained the realms of Brahma, Indra, and so forth, all these happy fruits of *samsaric* existence did not last. Now I shall ignore myself and, by every possible means, I shall lead all sentient beings as limitless as space to the unsurpassed happiness of liberation by freeing them from the sufferings of *samsara.*

And think further: How nice if all these mothers, who are deprived of happiness, experience happiness! May they come across happiness! By every means I shall let them meet with happiness! How nice if all these mothers, who are tormented by suffering, were freed from suffering! May they be free from suffering! I shall free them from suffering! And that too I shall do by myself!

However, do you have the ability to accomplish this? Contemplate thus: At present, I do not have the ability to free even a single sentient being from the sufferings of *samsara* and lead them to unsurpassed happiness – not to mention all sentient beings. Nevertheless, I have made such a pledge. And now, if I were to renege on my pledge I would fall into the unfortunate realms of existence. No one except the Buddhas is able to free all sentient beings from suffering and lead them on to unsurpassed happiness. Therefore, whatever it may take, may I attain the state of complete and perfect Buddhahood in order to free all sentient beings from each and every suffering and lead them onward to unsurpassed happiness.

Training in the Causes that Prevent the Decline of Bodhicitta in this Life

It is not sufficient to have just this wish. In order for the motivation of *bodhicitta* not to decline in this life there are four causes to be trained in: Training in being mindful of the benefits of *bodhicitta* to increase enthusiasm: training in generating actual *bodhicitta* six times a day in order to increase it; training in not forsaking sentient beings for whom you have generated *bodhicitta* and training in accumulating merit.

1. The moment you generate *bodhicitta*, you become an object of worship for all humans and gods, you outshine the Hearer and Solitary Realizer Arahats in terms of lineage [of a Buddha], you are safe from harm by epidemics and evil spirits, you are able to easily accomplish pacifying activities and so forth, you will not be born in the unfortunate realms and so forth, or even if you are born there you will come out of these realms quickly and can instantly destroy even the most powerful unwholesome actions. As it is said that, were the benefits of *bodhicitta* to have form they would not fit in the sky, therefore you should think of developing this altruistic intention further, without degeneration.

2. Meanwhile, if you forsake *bodhicitta*, the ripening effect of this will be heavier than the moral defeat of a *bhikshu*. Hence, do not give up *bodhicitta* until you attain Buddhahood. And generate *bodhicitta* three times a day and three times each night by reciting the following verse three times during both the day and night:

> In the Buddha, Dharma and Sangha
> I seek refuge until I am enlightened.
> Through my practices of giving and so forth
> May I accomplish Buddhahood for the sake of all sentient beings.

3. Since you have generated *bodhicitta* for the sake of all sentient beings, no matter how sentient beings behave [towards you], think that, on your part, you will never ever give up on them.

4. In order not to degenerate – but advance the *bodhicitta* which you have generated this once – you should train in accumulating vast merit by making offerings to the Three Jewels and so forth.

Training in the Causes for Preventing the Loss of Bodhicitta in Future Lives

As for the causes for preventing the loss of *bodhicitta* in future lives also, you should train in abandoning the four dark practices and relying on the four light practices. The four dark practices are as follows:

First, since trying to deceive any honored person – such as an abbot, spiritual teacher and so on – by lying to him constitutes dark practices, you should never do such a thing. As an antidote to it, do not lie to any sentient being, even at the cost of your life or in jest.

The second dark practice is to cause others to regret their virtuous practices which they do not otherwise regret. Never do such a thing and, as an antidote to it, lead your disciples – who need you to be spiritually mature – not into Hinayana but to Mahayana, if they prove to be worthy vessels for this.

The third dark practice is criticizing, out of hatred, someone who has developed the Mahayana attitude of *bodhicitta*. You should never do this, and to counteract this behavior perceive those on the Mahayana path as Buddhas. Whenever the occasion arises, duly praise them for their qualities. Moreover, train in the pure vision of all sentient beings.

The fourth dark practice is interacting with sentient beings with conceit or deception. You should never do this and always be honest with sentient beings. The Venerable Master says:

> *Bodhicitta* is the trunk of the tree of the Supreme Vehicle's path
> The foundation and basis of the great practices.
> It is like an elixir for the Two Accumulations
> It is a treasury of merit containing countless virtues.
> Knowing this, the courageous Children of the Victors
> Hold this precious, supreme aspiration as their core practice.

10

Training in the Practices of Engaging Bodhicitta

So, is it sufficient only to train in the aspiring *bodhicitta*? No, it is not sufficient. Additionally, you should take the vows of engaging *bodhicitta* and train in the great deeds of Bodhisattvas which are the Six Perfections, to ripen your own mind-stream, and the Four Ways of Gathering Disciples, to ripen the mind-streams of others.

How to Train in the Six Perfections

1. Training in the Perfection of Generosity

Motivated by the thought of accomplishing Buddhahood for the benefit of all sentient beings, give the true sacred teachings of the Buddha to all who have not received them; protect others from the threats of kings, battles and so forth; protect others from the dangers of animate beings such as demons, wild animals, snakes and the dangers of inanimate phenomena such as fire and water; and to the destitute give food, drink, medicines and so forth without feeling a sense of loss. In brief, give your body, possessions and all the roots of virtue that you have accumulated in three times [past, present and future] without feeling any deprivation. The Venerable Master says thus:

> Generosity is the wish-fulfilling gem that satisfies the hopes of wanderers
> The superior weapon that cuts the knot of meanness
> The *bodhisattva* deed that generates unfailing courage

And the foundation of glory that roars in the ten directions.
Knowing this, the learned ones cultivate the noble path
Of giving one's body, possessions and virtues.

2. Training in the Perfection of Ethics

You should attain Buddhahood for the benefit of all sentient beings. For this reason, with steady mindfulness and conscientiousness and a sense of self-reproach and embarrassment, do not commit unwholesome actions even at the cost of your life. Through such ethics of refraining from misdeeds, enhance the Six Perfections. Based on these two [ethics] you should succeed in faultlessly benefiting sentient beings. Thus, train in the three ethics. The Venerable Master advises:

Ethics is the water that cleanses the stains of misdeeds
The moonlight that soothes the tormenting heat of delusions.
One stands majestically like Meru amidst sentient beings
Without intimidation all beings bow down to you.
Knowing this, the worthy ones guard
Their well-accepted ethics like their eyes.

3. Training in the Perfection of Patience

When others harm you it is not right to react with anger because the harm they cause you is a karmic effect of the harm you did to them in the past. And also, since they are uncontrollably overpowered by anger, you should not harm them in return. Moreover, even a moment of anger destroys the roots of virtue of the three fundamental practices[15] accumulated over many eons. Hence, think, "I will not have even an inkling of anger in my mind", and practice the patience of remaining undisturbed by harm in your heart of hearts.

The experience of intense suffering caused by others hurting you eliminates your pride, arrogance and so forth, and generates renunciation of *samsara*. So when you experience unwanted suffering it has resulted from an unwholesome action, and you understand that a result cannot arise without a cause; therefore you will not engage in unwholesome actions. By practicing patience in response to the hurt caused by others and by completing the rest of the Six Perfections you will become a Buddha. Thus, you should see those who hurt you as spiritual teachers who give you instructions for cultivating patience, and feel grateful to them. Hence, in your heart of hearts practice the patience of accepting suffering.

By seeing the inconceivable powers of the Three Jewels, Buddhas and Bodhisattvas, you will develop the wish to train in the *bodhisattva* deeds and the understanding of selflessness that comes from believing in them. Thus, practice the patience of believing in the truth of Dharma from the depths of your heart. The Venerable Master says:

> Patience is the finest ornament of the Powerful Ones
> The best ascetic practice for the tormenting afflictions
> The garuda, the enemy of the snake of hatred
> The stout armor against the weapons of harsh speech.
> Knowing this, by various means
> They cultivate the excellent armor of patience.

5. Training in the Perfection of Joyous Effort

Those who are attached to base pleasures, such as remaining idle through the three doors [of body, speech and mind], sexual intercourse, sleep and so forth — because they do not contemplate the sorrowful state of *samsara* — become lazy. Hence, you should get rid of the causes of laziness and devote your body, speech and mind solely to wholesome practices.

The armor-like joyous effort is the intention to engage in austere practices such as removing the sufferings of just even a single sentient being, even if this means disregarding your body or life. Then, the practice of the joyous effort of gathering virtues is the enhancement of the practices of the Six Perfections. Then, based on these two, the joyous effort of benefiting sentient beings is to strive to serve their impeccable interests. You should pursue these joyous efforts as the Venerable Master says:

> If one dons the armor of unwavering joyous effort
> The virtues of scriptural knowledge and insight will increase
> like the waxing moon
> All activities will become meaningful
> Every work begun will be accomplished as desired.
> Knowing this, the Bodhisattvas practice great joyous effort
> That dispels all laziness.

5. Training in the Perfection of Concentration

Motivated by *bodhicitta* you should train in the following concentrations, free from laxity and excitement: The two mundane and supramundane concentrations; the three concentrations distinguished on the basis of their aspects of calm abiding, insight, and the union of calm abiding and insight; and the three concentrations defined in terms of their functions – the concentration that helps the body and mind remain in a blissful state in this life, the concentration that helps accomplish higher qualities such as clairvoyance, and the concentration that helps accomplish the welfare of sentient beings. The Venerable Master also says:

> Meditative concentration is the king that rules the mind
> When remaining focused it is immovable like the King of Mountains
> When directed it engages with all the objects of the virtuous mind
> And induces functional bliss for the body and mind.
> Knowing this, the great yogis always rely upon *samadhi*,
> The destroyer of the enemy of mental distractions.

6. Training in the Perfection of Wisdom

Motivated by *bodhicitta* you should train in the following aspects of wisdom: The wisdom of realizing the ultimate truth, reality as it is, which eliminates the root of *samsara*; the wisdom of realizing the conventional truth; and the wisdom that is engaged for the benefit of sentient beings with the help of the former two wisdoms. The Venerable Master also said:

> Wisdom is the eye through which to see profound reality
> The path that eliminates the root of samsara
> The treasury of virtues praised in all the scriptures
> Renowned as the excellent lamp that dispels the darkness
> of ignorance.
> Knowing this, the learned ones who seek liberation
> Dedicate every effort to generate the path.

How to Train in the Four Ways of Gathering Disciples

Motivated by the intention of attaining Buddhahood for the sake of sentient beings, first of all – through the practice of generosity of giving material things – you should gather sentient beings around you. Then, you should show them a smiling face in order to delight them and, having done that, make them feel relaxed by speaking gently to them. Then teach them the Dharma, such as the Six Perfections, in a sweet voice. Then let them practice the teachings; that is, let them follow the teachings according to what you have taught them. And be consistent in your practice, which means you should practice the Six Perfections yourself just as you ask others to practice. So, whatever it takes, you should train in these four profound methods of accomplishing benefits for the sake of others.

11

How to Specifically Train in the Last Two Perfections

As self-grasping is the root of *samsara*, without meditating on the path that directly contradicts its mode of apprehending an object, mere single-pointed concentration cannot eliminate the root of *samsara*. And without the single-pointed calm abiding – which keeps its focus unwaveringly – the mere wisdom of realizing the lack of true existence [of phenomena] cannot eliminate the root of *samsara*, however much you may analyze [the object of meditation]. This is because, in order to attain liberation – the eradication of mental afflictions – you must expand the intelligence that realizes reality-as-it-is through the wisdom that correctly engages the meaning of reality-as-it-is. The perfect view of realization of emptiness, that resolves the correct mode of the being of things, must be mounted on the horse of calm abiding which does not waver from its object; and with the sharp weapons of the four great reasonings of the Middle Way, free from the extremes of eternalism and nihilism, [the perfect view] destroys all of the objectifications of the extreme views. The Venerable Master says:

> Single-pointed concentration alone
> Is seen as powerless to eliminate the root of samsara.
> Insight devoid of the path of calm abiding
> Cannot overcome the afflictions, however much it analyzes.
> Hence, the insight that resolves the mode of being of things
> Should mount the horse of unwavering calm abiding

And through the sharp weapon of Madhyamika reasoning, free
from extremes
All the extreme graspings are destroyed.
With the vast insight that correctly analyzes thus
The intelligence that realizes reality is expanded.

By placing the mind single-pointedly on an object of focus, without wavering, the stabilized concentration of calm abiding is achieved. Moreover, while remaining in this single-pointed concentration, a firm stabilized concentration, unmoved from its object – the meaning of emptiness, reality-as-it-is – is generated through the correct analysis of the meaning of reality with discriminative wisdom. Seeing this, think how wonderful it is to put effort into accomplishing the union of calm abiding and special insight, and making this as an object of your prayer strive to imprint it within you. The Venerable Master says:

Single-pointed familiarization evidently brings
meditative concentration
Yet the correct analysis of the mode of being of things
By the [insight of] individual investigation
Also generates meditative concentration that remains
firm and unwavering.
Seeing this, how marvelous are those who strive to accomplish
Such a union of calm abiding and special insight!

Stay absorbed in such a meditative equipoise of the union of calm abiding and special insight, single-pointedly focused on the space-like emptiness which is absent of all extremes of elaboration. Then, coming out from this, you should meditate on the illusion-like emptiness of the post-meditative period when things appear as if they exist inherently though they do not. Then, suffused with compassion and *bodhicitta,* reaching the other shore of *bodhisattva* deeds through the practice of the union of method and wisdom, you become worthy of praise. Understanding this, being discontented with the dual paths of only either method or wisdom, training in the path of the union of method and wisdom is the tradition of the fortunate beings. Hence, one should make such effort, as the Venerable Master says:

> Meditating on the space-like emptiness of meditative equipoise
> And the illusion-like emptiness of the post-meditation state
> And engaging in the practices of Bodhisattvas
> Through the union of method and wisdom, is praiseworthy.
> Understanding this, not being satisfied with the partial path
> Is the tradition of the Fortunate Ones.

12

How to Specifically Train in the Vajrayana

Thus, having trained well in the paths common to *Sutra* and *Tantra* you must unquestionably enter into *Tantra*. The way of doing this is: First, you should ripen your mind-stream through being granted empowerments from a qualified *vajra* master, as prescribed in the *Tantras*. Then you should properly keep the pledges and vows taken at the time of the empowerments and train in the yoga with signs and the yoga without signs, in the case of the three lower *Tantras*, and train in the Two Stages sequentially in the case of the highest *yoga tantra*. Thus you will train yourself in the complete body of the path comprising all the key paths of *Sutra* and *Tantra*, and make it meaningful to have obtained a human rebirth with leisure and endowment. And this is how you should bring the precious teachings of the Buddha within the mind-streams of yourself and others.

The Venerable Master practiced just like this, and he advises his followers such as you to do likewise. Reflecting this, visualize the Venerable Master before you and think that he is joyfully instructing us in a clear voice, and actually reciting the lines, feeling moved by them. Thus imagine that the Venerable Master instructs you:

> Thus, generating the common path, which is essential for both
> The Causal and Resultant Vehicles of Mahayana
> And then, through a proficient captain's guidance
> Entering into the ocean of *Tantras*
> And receiving the complete quintessential instruction

Is the way to make human rebirth meaningful.
I, a yogi, practiced in this way.
You, who seek liberation, should do likewise.

In order to make familiar in my own mind
And also to benefit other fortunate beings
I have herein explained in an easy manner
The complete path that pleases the Victors.
I pray and dedicate any merit thus created
For all sentient beings not to be separated
from the pure and noble path.
I, a yogi, practiced in this way.
You, who seek liberation, should do likewise.

Having done this, you should recite the verses of dedication below and others from the depths of your heart:

From now onward, in this and future lives
Bless me to worship you at your lotus feet.
Bless me to listen to your teachings
And bless me to only please you with all my activities of the three doors.

And, "Throughout my lifetimes may the Victorious Tsongkhapa..." and so forth.

Dedication

May this succinct and flawless core instruction
On the paths of the *Lamrim*, the essence
of the instructions
Of Venerable Dipamkara and Tsongkhapa
Lead all beings along the path that pleases the Buddhas.

Colophon

This The Essence of Superfine Gold: A Guide on the Stages of the Path of the Beings of Three Capacities is written in an easy and compresensible manner in conjunction with the Venerable Master's A Song of Experience. It is written at the persistent request of Dochoe Choeje – a great illuminator of the Dharma who has immense faith and interest in this tradition – the great abbot of the monastery of Omniscient Sherab Pelzang. It is written by the Shakya Bhikshu Sonam Gyatso – who has seen signs of being blessed by the Venerable Master since a tender age – in his room, the Swirling Sunbeam, in the Palace of Sublime Joy at the great monastic center of Drepung. May this composition be able to spread the essence of the teaching in all directions always! May it be auspicious!

Notes

1 The three times are past, present and future

2 The beings of three capacities are: A being of lesser capacity, a being of medium capacity and a being of great capacity

3 Literally it means the Sumatran. He is also known by the names Dharmakirtishri and Maitripada

4 Je Tsongkhapa (1357-1419)

5 Authored by Je Tsongkhapa

6 Authored by Atisha Dipamkara (982-1054)

7 The three faults of a vessel are: Being upside down, being dirty though held right side up, and having a leaky bottom though clean

8 The six attitudes are: Thinking of yourself as a sick person, thinking of the spiritual teacher as a doctor, thinking of the instructions of the spiritual teacher as medicine; thinking of earnest practice as the way to cure your disease, thinking of the Tathagata as an excellent being and wishing that the teaching of the Buddha will remain for a long time

9 The three scriptural collections are: The scriptural collection of disciplines, the scriptural collection of discourses and the scriptural collection of knowledge

10 The four immeasurables are: Immeasurable compassion, immeasurable love, immeasurable joy and immeasurable equanimity

11 The three-fold offerings are: Offering of wealth, offering of service and practice [in accordance with their instructions]

12 These two are famous examples: After Arya Asanga had meditated on Maitreya, the Bodhisattva appeared to him in the form of a maggot-ridden bitch. Maitreya appeared only after Asanga cleaned her maggots with his tongue. Tilopa was roasting fish when Naropa first encountered his future guru and thought him crazy.

13 Cyclic existence.

14 A herbal flower of the tree *aeschynomene grandiflora*.

15 The three fundamental practices of Vinaya are the bi-monthly confession, summer retreat and conclusion of the summer retreat

༄༅། །བྱང་ཆུབ་ལམ་གྱི་རིམ་པའི་ཁྲིད་
བདུད་རྩི་གསེར་གྱི་ཡང་ཞུན་
བཞུགས་སོ།།

རྒྱལ་བ་སྐུ་ཕྲེང་གསུམ་པ་བསོད་ནམས་རྒྱ་མཚོ།

༄རྒྱལ་བ་སྐུ་ཕྲེང་གསུམ་པ་བསོད་ནམས་རྒྱ་མཚོའི་རྣམ་ཐར་མདོར་བསྡུས།

༄རྒྱལ་བ་སྐུ་ཕྲེང་གསུམ་པ་བསོད་ནམས་རྒྱ་མཚོ་ནི། ལྷ་ས་སྐྱིད་ཤོད་སྟོད་ལུང་ཁང་གསར་གོང་དུ་ཡབ་སྡེ་པ་རྣམ་རྒྱལ་གྲགས་པ་དང་། ཡུམ་དཔལ་འཛོམས་བུ་ཁྲིད་གཉིས་ཀྱི་སྲས་སུ་ཆུ་ཡོས་(༡༥༤༣)ལོར་གྲོད་བཏུམས་ཀྱི་ནང་ནས་འཁྲུངས་ཤིང་། ཤེལ་ལྟར་དཀར་ཞིང་དྭངས་པའི་གྲོད་པའི་ནང་དུ་བཞུགས་པ་ཉི་འོད་ཀྱིས་པདྨ་བྱེ་བ་ལྟར་འཁྲུངས་མ་ཐག་ངང་གིས་གྲོད་པ་བྱེ་ནས་ཤེལ་ལྟར་དྭངས་པའི་སྐུ་བལྟ་བས་ཆོག་མི་ཤེས་པ་མཚན་དཔེ་དང་ལྡན་པ་ཞིག་བྱོན་ནོ། །དེའི་ཚེ་ནམ་མཁའི་ཁྱོན་ཐམས་ཅད་འཇའ་གུར་གྱིས་གང་ཞིང་ལྷ་རྣམས་ཀྱིས་མེ་ཏོག་གི་ཆར་ཕབ། འཁྲུངས་མ་ཐག་ར་མ་དཀར་མོའི་འོ་མ་ཞལ་དུ་གསོལ་བ་དང་ཡབ་ཡུམ་གཉིས་ཀྱིས་ཤེས་པ་བརྗོད་ཅིང་ར་ནུ་སྲི་ཆོད་དཔལ་བཟང་པོ་ཞེས་མཚན་གསོལ། འཁྲུངས་ཙམ་ཉིད་ནས་མ་ཎི་ཞལ་འདོན་དུ་མཛད་པ་ཞིག་བྱུང་ཞིང་ཐ་མལ་གྱི་སྤྱོད་པ་ཐམས་ཅད་ལས་འདས་ཏེ་ཆོས་འཆད་པའི་ཕྱག་རྒྱ་དང་། ཏིང་ངེ་འཛིན་ལ་བཞུགས་པའི་ཚུལ་མཛད།།

དགུང་ལོ་གསུམ་ཙམ་ནས་སྐུ་གོང་མའི་མཛད་པ་རྣམ་ཐར་རྗེས་སུ་དྲན་ཏེ་དེ་དང་དེའི་ངང་ཚུལ་ཁོ་ན་མཛད་ཅིང་། ཞལ་ནས་ཀྱང་དེ་བཞིན་དུ་གསུང་བ་ཞིག་བྱུང་བས་ཕྱོགས་ཐམས་ཅད་དུ་རྒྱལ་བ་དགེ་འདུན་རྒྱ་མཚོའི་སྤྲུལ་སྐུ་ར་གྲགས། དགུང་ལོ་བཞི་ལ་ཕེབས་སྐབས་ཕྱག་བྲིས་འབྲི་ཀློག་སོགས་ལ་བརྩོན་པར་མཛད་པའི་ལོ་དེ་ར་འབྲས་སྤུངས་དགའ་ལྡན་ཕོ་བྲང་གི་གསེར་ཁྲི་ར་ཕེབས། པཎ་ཆེན་བསོད་ནམས་གྲགས་པའི་

(༡༤༧༨-༡༥༥༤) དྲུང་ནས་ཡོངས་རྫོགས་དགེ་བསྙེན་གྱི་སྡོམ་པ་བཞེས་ཏེ་མཚན་བསོད་ནམས་རྒྱ་མཚོ་དཔལ་བཟང་པོ་བསྟན་པའི་ཉི་མ་ཕྱོགས་ལས་རྣམ་རྒྱལ་དུ་གསོལ། དགུང་ལོ་ལྔ་ལ་སྐུ་གོང་མས་ཕྱི་ལོ་ ༡༥༠༨ ལོར་ཕྱག་བཏབ་པའི་ཆོས་འཁོར་རྒྱལ་མེ་ཏོག་ཐང་གི་དགོན་པར་ཕེབས། དེའི་ཚེ་དཔལ་ལྡན་དམག་ཟོར་མས་དགྱེས་པའི་ཚོ་འཕྲུལ་སྣ་ཚོགས་བསྟན་ཅིང་། རྒྱལ་གྱི་རྟེན་རྣམས་ལ་མཆོད་འབུལ་སྨོན་ལམ་དང་དགེ་འདུན་རྣམས་ལ་ཆོས་ཀྱི་བདུད་རྩི་སྩལ། དེ་ནས་ཚུར་འབྲས་སྤུངས་སུ་ཕེབས།།

དགུང་ལོ་བདུན་ཐོག་པཎ་ཆེན་བསོད་ནམས་གྲགས་པ་མཆོག་གི་སྐུ་དྲུང་ནས་དགེ་ཚུལ་གྱི་སྡོམ་པ་བཞེས་པ་དང་ཚེ་དབང་གྲུབ་རྒྱལ་མ་སོགས་ཀྱི་རྗེས་གནང་ཡང་གསན། གླིང་སྟོད་ཆོས་རྗེ་ལེགས་པའི་དོན་གྲུབ་དང་ཤར་རྩེ་ལེགས་པ་དོན་གྲུབ་དྲུང་ནས་མདོ་སྔགས་ཀྱི་ཟབ་ཆོས་མང་པོའི་ལུང་གསན། དེ་རྣམས་ཀྱི་དོན་ཐམས་ཅད་ཐོས་བསམ་གྱིས་གཏན་ལ་འབེབས་པ་དང་ཉམས་བཞེས་མཛད་དོ། །དེ་ནས་རྒྱལ་དང་འབྲས་སྤུངས་གཉིས་རེས་མོས་སུ་བཞུགས་ཤིང་ལམ་བར་གྱི་ཆོས་སྡེ་རྣམས་སུ་གསུང་ཆོས་ཀྱང་སྩལ། དགུང་ལོ་བདུན་ཡན་ལ་ཚེ་དཔག་མེད་ཀྱི་སྔགས་འབུམ་ཕྲག་བཅུ་གསུམ། དབྱངས་ཅན་མའི་བསྙེན་པ་ས་ཡ་ལྔ་། སྐྱབས་འགྲོ་འབུམ་ཕྲག་བཞི་བཅས་གྲུབ་པར་མཛད།།

དགུང་ལོ་བཅུ་པ་ཆུ་བྱི་ (༡༥༥༢) ལོར་འབྲས་སྤུངས་ཀྱི་ཁྲི་ཐོག་བཅུ་གཉིས་པ་གནང་། དེའི་ཕྱི་ལོར་ལྷ་ལྡན་སྨོན་ལམ་ཆེན་མོའི་ཚོགས་དབུར་ཕེབས་ཏེ་སྔ་དྲོ་འཁྲུངས་རབས་སོ་བཞི་པའི་གཟབ་བཤད་དང་ཕྱི་དྲོ་སྨོན་ལམ་དང་བསྔོ་བ་མཛད་པ་སོགས་རྗེ་རིན་པོ་ཆེའི་མཛད་ཆེན་མ་ཉམས་པར་སྐྱོང་བར་མཛད། དེའི་ཚེ་དཀར་ཕྱོགས་ཀྱི་ལྷ་རྣམས་དགའ་བས་མེ་ཏོག་གི་ཆར་ཆེན་པོ་ཕབ་པ་སོགས་ངོ་མཚར་བསམ་གྱིས་མི་ཁྱབ་

པ་བྱུང་ངོ་། དགུང་ལོ་བཅུ་གཅིག་ཡན་ལ་གུར་དྲག་གི་སྔགས་འབུམ་ཕྲག་ཉིས་བརྒྱ་དང་། དགུང་ལོ་བཅུ་གསུམ་ལ་ཆོས་འཁོར་རྒྱལ་དུ་ཕེབས། དེར་ཡེ་ཤེས་ཁྱུང་ནག་གི་སྔགས་འབུམ་གཅིག་དང་འབྲས་སྤུངས་སུ་དམིགས་བརྩེ་མ་འབུམ་ཕྲག་བཞི་བཅས་གྲུབ་པར་མཛད།།

དགུང་ལོ་བཅུ་བཞི་མེ་འབྲུག་(༡༥༥༦)ལོར་ཡར་ཀླུང་སྣེ་གདོང་པ་དང་། འཕྱོངས་རྒྱས་ནང་སོ་མ་མཐུན་ཞིང་སྡེ་གཟར་ཆེ་བ་ལངས་པར་བར་འདུམ་དུ་ཕེབས་ཏེ་ཞི་འཛགས་བྱུང་བ་སོགས་ཀུན་གྱིས་སྨྲེ་མོས་ཆེ། དགུང་ལོ་བཅུ་དྲུག་ས་རྟ་(༡༥༥༨)ལོར་སེ་རའི་ཁྲི་ཐོག་བཅུ་གསུམ་པ་གནང་། ཕྱི་ལོར་སྣེ་གདོང་མི་དབང་བཀྲ་ཤིས་གྲགས་པ་རྒྱལ་མཚན་ནས་ཀུན་དེང་ཏའི་གུ་ཤྲི་ཏོང་ཏང་གི་མཚན་གནས་དང་། ཕྱག་དམ་དམར་པོ་གནང་ཆོག་པའི་བཀའ་ཤོག་ཕུལ། དེ་ནས་ལོ་གཉིས་རྗེས་ཆར་ཤུགས་ཆེས་ཆེར་རྒྱས་ཏེ་ལྷ་སར་ཆུ་ཉེན་ཆེན་པོ་བྱུང་རྐྱེན་དེའི་ཕྱི་ལོར་ལྷ་ལྡན་སྨོན་ལམ་ཆེན་མོའི་རྗེས་འབྲེལ་དགེ་འདུན་རྣམས་ནས་རྡོ་བོའི་རགས་རྡོ་སྐྱེལ་བའི་སྲོལ་བཟང་འཛུགས་པར་མཛད།།

ཉེར་གཅིག་སྐྱེང་ཁྲི་ཆེན་བདེ་བ་ཅན་པ་དགེ་ལེགས་དཔལ་བཟང་(༡༥༠༥-༡༥༦༧)གིས་མཁན་པོ་དང་། བསྟན་པ་དར་རྒྱས་ཀྱིས་ལས་སློབ། དགེ་འཕེལ་ཆོས་རྗེ་ཕྱོགས་ལས་རྣམ་རྒྱལ་བས་གསང་སྟོན། ལྷ་བཙུན་བསོད་ནམས་དཔལ་བཟང་གིས་དུས་བསྒྲོ་བ་མཛད་དེ་དགེ་སློང་གི་སྡོམ་པ་བཞེས། དེ་ནས་དགེ་བའི་བཤེས་གཉེན་ཀུན་བཟང་རྩེ་པ་དང་། དཔལ་ལྡན་ས་སྐྱ་པའི་བསྟན་འཛིན་ཆེན་པོ་ཚར་ཆེན་བློ་གསལ་རྒྱ་མཚོ། རྗེ་བདེ་བ་ཅན་པ་སོགས་མཁས་གྲུབ་དུ་མ་ལས་ཆོས་བཀའ་མང་པོ་དང་གཞུང་ཆེན་ལ་གསན་བསམ་མཛད།།

དགུང་ལོ་ཉེར་ལྔ་མེ་ཡོས་(༡༥༨༧)ལོར་བཀྲས་ལྷུན་གྲྭ་ཚང་བླ་མ་རྣམས་ཀྱིས་གཙང་ཕྱོགས་སུ་གདན་འདྲེན་ཞུས་ཏེ་སེར་སྐྱ་རྣམས་ལ་ཆོས་འཁོར་རྒྱ་ཆེར་བསྐོར། དེ་ནས་ལོ་གཉིས་རྗེས་ཆོས་འཁོར་རྒྱལ་གྱི་གདན་སའི་ཆོས་སྲུང་ཕྱི་ནང་གསང་གསུམ་གྱི་རྟེན་རྣམས་གསར་དུ་བཞེངས། དེ་ལྟར་རྗེ་འདི་བསྟན་པའི་དོན་དུ་ངལ་བ་མེད་པར་དབུས་གཙང་གི་སའི་ཆ་ཕལ་མོ་ཆེར་ཞབས་ཀྱིས་བཅགས་ནས་རྒྱལ་བའི་བསྟན་པ་ལ་མ་དད་པ་རྣམས་དད་པར་བྱས་ཤིང་དད་པ་རྣམས་ལྷག་པར་དད་པ་འཕེལ་བར་བྱས། གཙོ་བོར་འབྲས་སྤུངས་དང་རྒྱལ་གཉིས་གདན་ས་འདྲ་བར་མཛད་དེ་གཉིས་ཀར་རེས་མོས་ཀྱིས་བཞུགས་ཤིང་ཆོས་དང་ཟང་ཟིང་གཉིས་ཀའི་སྒོ་ནས་ལེགས་པར་བསྐྱངས།།

དགུང་ལོ་སོ་གཉིས་ཤིང་ཁྲི་(༡༥༧༩)ལ་ཕན་བདེ་ལེགས་བཤད་སླིང་ཕྱུག་བཏབ། དེ་ནས་ལོ་གཉིས་རྗེས་སོག་པོ་ཨལ་ཐན་ཆོས་ཀྱི་རྒྱལ་པོས་སོག་ཡུལ་དུ་གདན་དྲངས་པར་རེ་ཞིག་སྐུ་ཚབ་ཏུ་འདུལ་བ་བླ་མ་བརྩོན་འགྲུས་བཟང་པོ་གཏོང་བར་མཛད། དེའི་ཕྱི་ལོར་ཆོས་རྒྱལ་ཨལ་ཐན་གྱིས་སྤྱན་འདྲེན་སྔ་ཕྱིར་ཞུས་པ་བཞིན་བྱང་ཕྱོགས་སོག་ཡུལ་དུ་བསྟན་པ་རིན་པོ་ཆེ་སྤེལ་བར་ཆིབས་ཁ་བསྒྱུར། རྭ་སྒྲེང་ནས་ཆིབས་ཐོག་ཏུ་འཁྱོལ་ཁར། ས་སྐྱོང་བཀྲ་ཤིས་རབ་བརྟན་པས་ཆིབས་ཡོབ་ལ་འཇུས་ནས། བསྟན་པའི་དཔལ་གྱུར་བླ་མའི་ཞབས་པད་བརྟན། །བསྟན་འཛིན་སྐྱེས་བུ་ས་སྟེང་ཡོངས་ལ་ཁྱབ། །ཅེས་ཚིག་རྐང་གཉིས་འཕྲུལ་རྩོམ་མཛད་ཐོག མཆི་མས་བརླངས་ཏེ་གསུང་རྒྱ་མ་བྱུང་བས། བསྟན་པའི་སྦྱིན་བདག་མངའ་ཐང་འབྱོར་པ་རྒྱས། །བསྟན་པ་ཡུན་རིང་གནས་པའི་བཀྲ་ཤིས་ཤོག །ཅེས་ཆིབས་ཐོག་ནས་གནང་བས་ཚིག་དོན་ཟབ་ཅིང་བྱིན་རླབས་ཆེ་བར་གྲགས།།

དེ་ནས་ཆིབས་པར་བསྐྱོད་དེ་འབྲི་ཆུ་ཁར་ཕེབས་པ་ལྷ་འདྲེའི་ཆོ་འཕྲུལ་གྱིས

འབྲི་ཆུ་སློ་བུར་དུ་འཁྲུགས་ཤིང་གཡོ་བས་ཕན་ཚུན་དུ་བགྲོད་དཀའ་བ་ལ། ཁྲི་བོའི་ལྷ་སྐུངས་དང་ཕྱོགས་མཛུབ་མཛད་པ་ཙམ་གྱིས་མི་ཕྱུགས་མཐའ་དག་བདེ་བར་བགྲོད་ཆོག་པ་བྱུང་། དེ་ནས་རིམ་གྱིས་ཉ་མཚོ་སྟོད་དུ་ཕེབས། དགོན་པས་གཙོས་པའི་སྐྱ་སེར་གྱི་ཁྲིམ་ཆེན་པོ་འཚོགས་ཏེ། གསེར་སྲང་སྟོང་ཕྲག་གསུམ་ཙམ་གྱིས་གཙོས་པའི་ཟང་ཟིང་གི་འབུལ་བ་རྒྱ་ཆེར་ཕུལ། བླ་མའི་རྣལ་འབྱོར་དང་ཡི་གེ་དྲུག་པའི་བཟླས་ལུང་། རབ་བྱུང་བསྙེན་རྫོགས་སྟོང་ཕྲག་ཏུ་ཉེ་བ་སོགས་གནང་སྟེ་ཀུན་ཀྱང་ཐར་པའི་ལམ་ལ་བཀོད།།

དེ་ནས་རྨ་ཆུའི་འགྲམ་དུ་བཞུགས་སྐབས་ཕེབས་པ་ན། ཚུར་མཐོང་གི་སྐྱེ་བོ་རྣམས་ཆུ་འདི་ཧ་ཅང་ཆེ་བས་རེ་ཞིག་སྒྲོལ་བར་མི་ནུས་སོ་ཞེས་སྨྲས་པ་ལ། སང་ནམ་ལངས་ཏེ་ལྷས་ཅན་དོང་པུས་ནུབ་ཙམ་ལས་མི་འདུག་པས་ཐམས་ཅད་སྨྲ་མི་ཤེས་པའི་ཡ་མཚན་དུ་གྱུར། དེ་ནས་རིམ་གྱིས་ཨ་རིག་དཀར་པོ་ཐང་དུ་བཞུགས་སྐབས་བཏེག་སྐབས་ཨ་རིག་རྣམས་ཀྱིས་ཧ་སྟོང་ཕྲག་དང་ཕྱུགས་ཁྲི་ཚོར་ཉེ་བའི་འབུལ་བ་ཕུལ། འཇའ་འོད་ཀྱི་གུར་དང་ལྷའི་མེ་ཏོག་གི་ཆར་བབས། སྐྱེ་བོ་མཐའ་དག་ལ་ཐར་པའི་ས་བོན་བསྐྲུན་པར་མཛད། དེ་ནས་ཐུར་ཨལ་ཐན་རྒྱལ་པོའི་བླ་མཆོད་དུ་རྫོང་ཏ་གནང་བའི་ཆོས་རྗེ་བརྩོན་འགྲུས་བཟང་པོ་དང་། ཡོ་ཙྪ་བ་གཱི་ཤྲཱི་གཉིས་ཀྱིས་གཙོས་པའི་ཧ་པ་ལྔ་བརྒྱ་སྙེར་རྒྱལ་པོའི་གམ་ནས་བསུ་བ་ལ་འབྱོར།།

དགུང་ལོ་སོ་དྲུག་ས་སྟག (༡༥༧༨) ལོར་ཆོས་རྒྱལ་ཨལ་ཐན་དང་མཇལ་ནས་དབུ་བླར་གྱུར་ཏེ་རྗེ་མཆོག་ལ་མི་རིགས་མི་གཅིག་པ་དྲུ་མའི་དབུས་སུ་གསེར་ལས་གྲུབ་པའི་དབུ་རྒྱན་དང་། བུམ་པ། རིགས་ལྔའི་ཕྱག་མཚན། གསེར་སྲང་བརྒྱ་ལས་གྲུབ་པའི་ཐམ་ཀ་ཁ་རིས་ལ། རྡོ་རྗེ་འཆང་ཏཱ་ལའི་བླ་མའི་ཐམ་ཀ་རྒྱལ་ཞེས་པ་ཞིག་དང་།

ཏཱ་ལའི་བླ་མ་བཛྲཀྵར་ཞེས་ཁྲབ་བདག་རྡོ་རྗེ་འཆང་གི་མཚན་བསྟོད་ཕུལ། དེ་ནས་བཟུང་རྒྱལ་དབང་སྐུ་ཕྲེང་རིམ་བྱོན་ལ་ཏཱ་ལའི་བླ་མ་ཞེས་པའི་མཚན་སྙན་གྲགས། རྒྱལ་དབང་མཆོག་ནས་ཨལ་ཐན་ལ་ཆོས་ཀྱི་རྒྱལ་པོ་ལྷའི་ཚངས་པ་ཞེས་པའི་མཚན་གནང་། སོག་ཡུལ་ལ་དམ་པའི་ཆོས་རྒྱ་ཆེར་བསྐོར། སོག་པོ་བརྒྱ་ཕྲག་མང་པོ་རབ་ཏུ་བྱུང་། ཕྱུགས་སྲོག་བསད་ནས་མཆོད་པའི་ལམ་སྲོལ་བཅོས་པར་མཛད། ཕྱི་ལོར་སོག་ཡུལ་དུ་བྱང་ཆེན་ཆོས་འཁོར་གླིང་ཕྱག་བཏབ།།

དགུང་ལོ་སོ་བརྒྱད་ལྕགས་འབྲུག་(༡༥༨༠)ལོར་ལི་ཐང་དུ་དགའ་ལྡན་ཐུབ་བསྟན་ཆོས་འཁོར་གླིང་དགོན་གྱི་བྱང་སེམས་ཆོས་རྗེའི་ཁྲིར་ཕེབས་ཏེ་སེར་སྐྱ་ཡོངས་ལ་ཆོས་ཀྱི་འཁོར་ལོ་རྒྱ་ཆེར་བསྐོར་བར་མཛད། སྐུ་འབུམ་བྱམས་པ་གླིང་རྒྱས་འདེབས་ཕྱོགས་སུ་ཕེབས་ནས་བཀའ་ཆོས་དུ་མ་གནང་། དགུང་ལོ་ཞེ་གཅིག་སྟེང་རྒྱལ་བ་ཙོང་ཁ་པ་སྐུ་བལྟམས་པའི་གནས་ཆེན་སྐུ་འབུམ་དུ་ཕེབས་ཏེ་བཤད་གྲྭ་འཛུགས་པའི་ཞལ་བཀོད་མཛད། ལོ་དེར་ཆོས་རྒྱལ་ཨལ་ཐན་སྐུ་གཤེགས་པ་དང་། དེའི་སྲས་ཀྱིས་གདན་དྲངས་པ་བཞིན་ཤིང་སྤྲེལ་(༡༥༨༩)ལོར་སོག་ཡུལ་དུ་བསྐྱར་ཕེབས་གནང་སྟེ་སོག་པོ་ནང་འཁྲུག་པ་འདུམ་འགྲིག་མཛད་པས་ཀུན་བདེ་ལ་འཁོད། ཤིང་བྱ་(༡༥༨༥)ལོར་སེ་ཆེན་ཏའི་ཆིང་གི་སྡེ་ཐོག་ཏུ་ཕེབས་ཏེ་ཕུན་ཚོགས་དར་རྒྱལ་གླིང་གི་དགོན་པ་ཕྱག་བཏབ།།

རྗེ་འདིས་ཕྱི་རབས་ཀྱི་གདུལ་བྱ་རྣམས་ཀྱི་དོན་དུ་བྱང་ཆུབ་ལམ་གྱི་རིམ་པའི་འཁྲིད་གསེར་གྱི་ཡང་ཞུན་མཛད་ཅིང་། གཞན་ཡང་གསོལ་འདེབས་བསྟོད་ཚོགས་དང་ཉམས་མགུར་སོགས་མང་དུ་ཡོད་དོ།།

དགུང་ལོ་ཞེ་དྲུག་ལ་ཕེབས་པ་ས་བྱི་(༡༥༨༨)ལོར་གོང་མ་མིང་ཧྲིན་ཙུང་གིས་སོག་ཡུལ་ནས་རྗེ་འདི་ཉིད་པེ་ཅིང་དུ་གདན་ཞུ་བྱས་པ་བཞིན་ཞལ་བཞེས་གནང་

ནས་པེ་ཅིང་ཕྱོགས་སུ་ཕེབས་ཉེ་ཐོན། འོན་ཀྱང་སོག་ཡུལ་ཁ་ར་ཆིན་དུ་སྐུ་མྱ་ངན་ལས་འདའ་བའི་ཚུལ་བསྟན། སྐུའི་གུང་ཐལ་དཔལ་ལྡན་འབྲས་སྤུངས་སུ་གདན་དྲངས་ཏེ་དངུལ་སྡོང་རིན་པོ་ཆེར་བཞུགས།། །།

ལམ་རིམ་ཉམས་མགུར་[༡] བཞུགས་སོ།།

རྒྱལ་བ་ཙོང་ཁ་པ།

༄༅། །ཕུན་ཚོགས་དགེ་ལེགས་བྱེ་བས་བསྐྲུན་པའི་སྐུ།།
མཐའ་ཡས་འགྲོ་བའི་རེ་བ་སྐོང་བའི་གསུང་།།
མ་ལུས་ཤེས་བྱ་ཇི་བཞིན་གཟིགས་པའི་ཐུགས།།
ཤཱཀྱའི་གཙོ་བོ་དེ་ལ་མགོས་ཕྱག་འཚལ།།

ཟླ་མེད་སྟོན་པ་དེ་ཡི་སྲས་ཀྱི་མཆོག།
རྒྱལ་བའི་མཛད་པ་ཀུན་གྱི་ཁུར་བསྣམས་ནས།།
གྲངས་མེད་ཞིང་དུ་སྤྲུལ་པས་རྣམ་རོལ་པ།།
མི་ཕམ་འཇམ་པའི་དབྱངས་ལ་ཕྱག་འཚལ་ལོ།།

ཤིན་ཏུ་དཔག་པར་དཀའ་བ་རྒྱལ་བའི་ཡུམ།།
ཇི་བཞིན་དགོངས་པ་འགྲེལ་མཛད་འཛམ་གླིང་རྒྱན།།
ཀླུ་སྒྲུབ་ཐོགས་མེད་ཅེས་ནི་ས་གསུམ་ན།།
ཡོངས་སུ་གྲགས་པའི་ཞབས་ལ་བདག་ཕྱག་འཚལ།།

ཤིང་རྟ་ཆེན་པོ་གཉིས་ལས་[༢]ལེགས་བརྒྱུད་པའི།།
ཟབ་མོ་ལྟ་བ་རྒྱ་ཆེན་སྤྱོད་པའི་ལམ།།
མ་ནོར་ཡོངས་སུ་རྫོགས་པའི་གནད་བསྡུས་པའི།།
གདམས་པའི་མཛོད་འཛིན་མར་མེ་མཛད་ལ་འདུད།།

རབ་འབྱམས་གསུང་རབ་ཀུན་ལ་ལྟ་བའི་མིག།
སྐལ་བཟང་ཐར་པར་བགྲོད་པའི་འཇུག་ངོགས་མཆོག།
བརྩེ་བས་བསྐྱོད་པའི་ཐབས་མཁས་མཛད་པ་ཡིས།།
གསལ་མཛད་བཤེས་གཉེན་རྣམས་ལ་གུས་ཕྱག་འཚལ།།

འཛམ་གླིང་མཁས་པ་ཡོངས་ཀྱི་གཙུག་གི་རྒྱན།།
སྙན་པའི་བ་དན་འགྲོ་ན་ལྷང་ངེ་བ།།
ཀླུ་སྒྲུབ་ཐོགས་མེད་གཉིས་ལས་རིམ་བཞིན་དུ།།
ལེགས་བརྒྱུད་བྱང་ཆུབ་ལམ་གྱི་རིམ་པ་ནི།།
སྐྱེ་དགུའི་[༣] འདོད་དོན་མ་ལུས་སྐོང་བས་ན།།
གདམས་པ་རིན་ཆེན་དབང་གི་རྒྱལ་པོ་སྟེ།།
གཞུང་བཟང་སྟོང་གི་ཆུ་བོ་འདུ་བའི་ཕྱིར།།
དཔལ་ལྡན་ལེགས་པར་བཤད་པའི་རྒྱ་མཚོའང་ཡིན།།

བསྟན་པ་ཐམས་ཅད་འགལ་མེད་རྟོགས་པ་དང་།།
གསུང་རབ་མ་ལུས་གདམས་པར་འཆར་བ་དང་།།
རྒྱལ་བའི་དགོངས་པ་བདེ་བླག་རྙེད་པ་དང་།།
ཉེས་སྤྱོད་ཆེན་པོའི་གཡང་ས་ལས་ཀྱང་བསྲུངས[༤] །།

དེ་ཕྱིར་རྒྱ་བོད་མཁས་པའི་སྐྱེ་བོ་ནི།།
སྐལ་ལྡན་དུ་མས་བསྟེན་པའི་གདམས་པ་མཆོག།
སྐྱེས་བུ་གསུམ་གྱི་ལམ་གྱི་རིམ་པ་ཡིས།།
ཡིད་རབ་མི་འཕྲོག་དཔྱོད་ལྡན་སུ་ཞིག་ཡོད།།

གསུང་རབ་ཀུན་གྱི་སྙིང་པོ་བསྡུ་བསྡུ་བ།།
ཚུལ་འདི་ཐུན་རེ་སྟོན་དང་ཉན་པས་ཀྱང་།།
དམ་ཆོས་འཆད་དང་ཐོས་པའི་ཕན་ཡོན་ཚོགས།།
རླབས་ཆེན་སྡུད་པར་ངེས་པས་དེ་དོན་བསམ།།

དེ་ནས་འདི་ཕྱིའི་ལེགས་ཚོགས་ཇི་སྙེད་པའི།།
རྟེན་འབྲེལ་ལེགས་པར་འགྲིག་པའི་རྩ་བ་ནི།།
ལམ་སྟོན་བཤེས་གཉེན་དམ་པ་འབད་པ་ཡིས།།
བསམ་དང་སྦྱོར་བས་ཚུལ་བཞིན་བསྟེན་པ་རུ།།
མཐོང་ནས་སྲོག་གི་ཕྱིར་ཡང་མི་གཏོང་བར།།
བཀའ་བཞིན་སྒྲུབ་[༥]པའི་མཆོད་པས་མཉེས་པར་བྱེད།།
རྣལ་འབྱོར་ངས་ཀྱང་ཉམས་ལེན་དེ་ལྟར་བགྱིས[༦]།།
ཐར་འདོད་ཁྱེད་ཀྱང་དེ་བཞིན་བསྐྱང་འཚལ་ལོ།།

དལ་བའི་རྟེན་འདི་ཡིད་བཞིན་ནོར་ལས་ལྷག།
འདི་འདྲ་རྙེད་པ་ད་རེས་ཙམ་ཞིག་ཡིན།།
རྙེད་དཀའ་འཇིག་སླ་ནམ་མཁའི་གློག་དང་འདྲ།།
ཚུལ་འདི་བསམས་ནས་འཇིག་རྟེན་བྱ་བ་ཀུན།།
སྦྲུན་པ་[༧]པ་འཕྱུར་བ་བཞིན་དུ་རྟོགས་འགྱུར་ནས།།
ཉིན་མཚན་ཀུན་ཏུ་སྙིང་པོ་ལེན་པ་དགོས།།
རྣལ་འབྱོར་ངས་ཀྱང་ཉམས་ལེན་དེ་ལྟར་བགྱིས།།
ཐར་འདོད་ཁྱེད་ཀྱང་དེ་བཞིན་བསྐྱང་འཚལ་ལོ།།

ཞི་ནས་ངན་འགྲོར་མི་སྐྱེའི་གདེང་[8] མེད་ཅིང་།།
དེ་ཡི་འཇིགས་སྐྱོབས་དཀོན་མཆོག་གསུམ་དུ་ངེས།།
དེ་ཕྱིར་སྐྱབས་འགྲོ་ཤིན་ཏུ་བརྟན་[9]པ་དང་།།
དེ་ཡི་བསླབ་བྱ་ཉམས་པ་མེད་པར་བྱ།།
དེ་ཡང་དཀར་ནག་ལས་འབྲས་ལེགས་བསམས་ནས།།
བླང་དོར་ཚུལ་བཞིན་བསྒྲུབ་ལ་རག་ལས་སོ།།
རྣལ་འབྱོར་ངས་ཀྱང་ཉམས་ལེན་དེ་ལྟར་བགྱིས།།
ཐར་འདོད་ཁྱེད་ཀྱང་དེ་བཞིན་བསྐྱང་འཚལ་ལོ།།

ལམ་མཆོག་སྒྲུབ་ལ་མཚན་ཉིད་ཚང་བའི་རྟེན།།
མ་རྙེད་བར་དུ་ས་ཚོད་[10] མི་འོང་བས།།
དེ་ཡི་མ་ཚང་མེད་པའི་རྒྱུ་ལ་བསླབ།།
སྒོ་གསུམ་སྡིག་ལྟུང་དྲི་མས་སྦགས་པ་འདི།།
ལྷག་པར་ལས་སྒྲིབ་སྦྱོང་བ་གནད་ཆེ་བས།།
རྒྱུན་དུ་སྟོབས་བཞི་ཚང་བར་བསྟེན་[11]པ་གཅེས།།
རྣལ་འབྱོར་ངས་ཀྱང་ཉམས་ལེན་དེ་ལྟར་བགྱིས།།
ཐར་འདོད་ཁྱེད་ཀྱང་དེ་བཞིན་བསྐྱང་འཚལ་ལོ།།

སྡུག་བདེན་ཉེས་དམིགས་བསམ་ལ་མ་འབད་ན།།
ཐར་པ་དོན་གཉེར་ཇི་བཞིན་མི་སྐྱེ་ཞིང་།།
ཀུན་འབྱུང་འཁོར་བའི་འཇུག་རིམ་མ་བསམས་ན།།
འཁོར་བའི་རྩ་བ་གཅོད་ཚུལ་མི་ཤེས་པས།།

སྲིད་ལས་ངེས་འབྱུང་སྐྱོ་ཤས་བརྟེན་[༡༣]པ་དང་།།
འཁོར་བ་གང་གིས་བཅིངས་པ་ཤེས་པ་གཅེས།།
རྣལ་འབྱོར་ངས་ཀྱང་ཉམས་ལེན་དེ་ལྟར་བགྱིས།།
ཐར་འདོད་ཁྱེད་ཀྱང་དེ་བཞིན་བསྐྱང་འཚལ་ལོ།།

སེམས་བསྐྱེད་ཐེག་མཆོག་[༡༤]ལམ་གྱི་གཞུང་ཤིང་སྟེ།།
རླབས་ཆེན་སྤྱོད་པ་རྣམས་ཀྱི་གཞི་དང་རྟེན།།
ཚོགས་གཉིས་ཀུན་ལ་གསེར་འགྱུར་རྩི་ལྟ་བུ།།
རབ་འབྱམས་དགེ་ཚོགས་སྡུད་པའི་བསོད་ནམས་གཏེར།།
དེ་ལྟར་ཤེས་ནས་རྒྱལ་སྲས་དཔའ་བོ་རྣམས།།
རིན་ཆེན་སེམས་མཆོག་ཐུགས་དམ་མཐིལ་དུ་འཛིན།།
རྣལ་འབྱོར་ངས་ཀྱང་ཉམས་ལེན་དེ་ལྟར་བགྱིས།།
ཐར་འདོད་ཁྱེད་ཀྱང་དེ་བཞིན་བསྐྱང་འཚལ་ལོ།།

སྦྱིན་པ་འགྲོ་བའི་རེ་སྐོང་ཡིད་བཞིན་ནོར།།
སེར་སྣའི་མདུད་པ་གཅོད་པའི་མཚོན་ཆ་མཆོག
མ་ཞུམ་སྙིང་སྟོབས་བསྐྱེད་པའི་རྒྱལ་སྲས་སྤྱོད།།
སྙན་པའི་གྲགས་པ་ཕྱོགས་བཅུར་སྒྲོག་པའི་གཞི།།
དེ་ལྟར་ཤེས་ནས་ལུས་དང་ལོངས་སྤྱོད་དགེ།
ཡོངས་སུ་གཏོང་བའི་ལམ་བཟང་མཁས་པས་བསྟེན།།
རྣལ་འབྱོར་ངས་ཀྱང་ཉམས་ལེན་དེ་ལྟར་བགྱིས།།
ཐར་འདོད་ཁྱེད་ཀྱང་དེ་བཞིན་བསྐྱང་འཚལ་ལོ།།

ཚུལ་ཁྲིམས་ཉེས་སྤྱོད་དྲི་མ་འཁྲུད་པའི་ཆུ།།
ཉོན་མོངས་ཚ་གདུང་སེལ་བའི་ཟླ་བའི་འོད།།
སྐྱེ་དགུའི་[༧༤] དབུས་ནས་ལྷུན་པོ་ལྟ་བུར་བརྗིད།།
སྟོབས་ཀྱིས་བསྡིགས་པ་མེད་པར་འགྲོ་ཀུན་འདུད།།
དེ་ལྟར་ཤེས་ནས་ཡང་དག་བླངས་པའི་ཁྲིམས།།
དམ་པ་རྣམས་ཀྱིས་མིག་བཞིན་བསྲུང་བར་མཛད།།
རྣལ་འབྱོར་ངས་ཀྱང་ཉམས་ལེན་དེ་ལྟར་བགྱིས།།
ཐར་འདོད་ཁྱེད་ཀྱང་དེ་བཞིན་བསྐྱང་འཚལ་ལོ།།

བཟོད་པ་སྟོབས་ལྡན་རྣམས་ལ་རྒྱན་གྱི་མཆོག།
ཉོན་མོངས་གདུང་བའི་དཀའ་ཐུབ་ཀུན་གྱི་ཕུལ།།
ཞེ་སྡང་ལག་འགྲོའི་དགྲ་ལ་ནམ་མཁའ་ལྡིང་།།
ཚིག་རྩུབ་མཚོན་ལ་སྲ་བའི་གོ་ཆ་ཡིན།།
དེ་ལྟར་ཤེས་ནས་བཟོད་མཆོག་གོ་ཆ་ལ།།
རྣམ་པ་སྣ་ཚོགས་ཚུལ་གྱིས་གོམས་པར་མཛད།།
རྣལ་འབྱོར་ངས་ཀྱང་ཉམས་ལེན་དེ་ལྟར་བགྱིས།།
ཐར་འདོད་ཁྱེད་ཀྱང་དེ་བཞིན་བསྐྱང་འཚལ་ལོ།།

མི་ལྡོག་[༧༥] བརྟན་པའི་བརྩོན་འགྲུས་གོ་བགོས་ན།།
ལུང་རྟོགས་ཡོན་ཏན་ཡར་ངོའི་ཟླ་བཞིན་འཕེལ།།
སྤྱོད་ལམ་ཐམས་ཅད་དོན་དང་ལྡན་པར་འགྱུར[༧༦] །།
གང་བརྩམས་ལས་ཀྱི་མཐའ་རྣམས་ཡིད་བཞིན་འགྲུབ།།

དེ་ལྟར་ཤེས་ནས་ལེ་ལོ་ཀུན་སེལ་བའི།།
ལྷབས་ཆེན་བརྩོན་འགྲུས་རྒྱལ་སྲས་རྣམས་ཀྱིས་བརྩམས[༡༧]།།
རྣལ་འབྱོར་ངས་ཀྱང་ཉམས་ལེན་དེ་ལྟར་བགྱིས།།
ཐར་འདོད་ཁྱེད་ཀྱང་དེ་བཞིན་བསྐྱང་འཚལ་ལོ།།

བསམ་གཏན་སེམས་ལ་དབང་བསྒྱུར་[༡༨]རྒྱལ་པོ་སྟེ།།
བཞག་ན་གཡོ་མེད་རི་ཡི་དབང་པོ་བཞིན།།
བཏང་ན་དགེ་བའི་དམིགས་པ་ཀུན་ལ་འཇུག།
ལུས་སེམས་ལས་སུ་རུང་བའི་བདེ་ཆེན་འདྲེན།།
དེ་ལྟར་ཤེས་ནས་རྣལ་འབྱོར་དབང་པོ་རྣམས།།
རྣམ་གཡེང་དགྲ་འཇོམས་ཏིང་འཛིན་རྒྱུན་དུ་བསྟེན།།
རྣལ་འབྱོར་ངས་ཀྱང་ཉམས་ལེན་དེ་ལྟར་བགྱིས།།
ཐར་འདོད་ཁྱེད་ཀྱང་དེ་བཞིན་བསྐྱང་འཚལ་ལོ།།

ཤེས་རབ་ཟབ་མོའི་དེ་ཉིད་ལྟ་བའི་མིག།
སྲིད་པའི་རྩ་བ་དྲུངས་[༡༩]ནས་འབྱིན་པའི་ལམ།།
གསུང་རབ་ཀུན་ལས་བསྔགས་པའི་ཡོན་ཏན་གཏེར།།
གཏི་མུག་མུན་སེལ་སྒྲོན་མེ་མཆོག་ཏུ་གྲགས།།
དེ་ལྟར་ཤེས་ནས་ཐར་འདོད་མཁས་པ་ཡིས།།
ལམ་དེ་འབད་པ་དུ་མས་བསྐྱེད་པར་མཛད།།
རྣལ་འབྱོར་ངས་ཀྱང་ཉམས་ལེན་དེ་ལྟར་བགྱིས།།
ཐར་འདོད་ཁྱེད་ཀྱང་དེ་བཞིན་བསྐྱང་འཚལ་ལོ།།

རྩེ་གཅིག་བསམ་གཏན་ཙམ་ལ་འཕོར་བ་ཡི།།
རྩ་བ་གཅོད་པའི་ནུས་པ་མ་མཐོང་ཞིང་།།
ཞི་གནས་ལམ་དང་བྲལ་བའི་ཤེས་རབ་ཀྱིས།།
ཇི་ཙམ་དཔྱད་ཀྱང་ཉོན་མོངས་མི་ལྡོག[༣༠] པས།།
ཡིན་ལུགས་ཤུ་ཐག་ཆོད་པའི་ཤེས་རབ་དེ།།
གཡོ་མེད་ཞི་གནས་རྟ་ལ་བསྐྱོན་ནས་ནི།།
མཐའ་བྲལ་དབུ་མའི་རིགས་པའི་མཚོན་རྣོན་གྱིས།།
མཐར་འཛིན་དམིགས་གཏད་ཐམས་ཅད་འཇིག་བྱེད་པ།།
ཚུལ་བཞིན་སྤྱོད་པའི་ཡངས་པའི་ཤེས་རབ་ཀྱིས།།
དེ་ཉིད་རྟོགས་པའི་བློ་གྲོས་རྒྱས་པར་མཛོད།།
རྣལ་འབྱོར་ངས་ཀྱང་ཉམས་ལེན་དེ་ལྟར་བགྱིས།།
ཐར་འདོད་ཁྱེད་ཀྱང་དེ་བཞིན་བསྐྱང་འཚལ་ལོ།།

རྩེ་གཅིག་གོམས་[༣༡]པས་ཏིང་འཛིན་འགྲུབ་པར་ནི།།
སྨོས་པར་ཅི་འཚལ་ཚུལ་བཞིན་དཔྱོད་པ་ཡི།།
སོ་སོར་རྟོག་པ་ཡིས་ཀྱང་ཡིན་ལུགས་ལ།།
གཡོ་མེད་ཤིན་ཏུ་བརྟན་པར་གནས་པ་ཡི།།
ཏིང་འཛིན་བསྐྱེད་[༣༢]པར་མཐོང་ནས་ཞི་ལྷག་གཉིས།།
ཟུང་འབྲེལ་སྒྲུབ་ལ་བརྩོན་རྣམས་ཡ་མཚན་ནོ།།
རྣལ་འབྱོར་ངས་ཀྱང་ཉམས་ལེན་དེ་ལྟར་བགྱིས།།
ཐར་འདོད་ཁྱེད་ཀྱང་དེ་བཞིན་བསྐྱང་འཚལ་ལོ།།

མཉམ་གཞག[33]ནམ་མཁའ་ལྟ་བུའི་སྟོང་ཉིད་དང་།།
རྗེས་ཐོབ་སྒྱུ་མ་ལྟ་བུའི་སྟོང་པ་གཉིས།།
བསྒོམས་ནས་ཐབས[34]ཤེས་ཟུང་དུ་འབྲེལ་བ་ཡིས།།
རྒྱལ་སྲས་སྤྱོད་པའི་ཕ་རོལ་འགྲོ་བ་བསྔགས།།
དེ་ལྟར་རྟོགས་ནས་ཕྱོགས་རེའི་ལམ་གྱིས་ནི།།
ཚིམ་པ་མེད་པ་སྐལ་བཟང་རྣམས་ཀྱི་ལུགས།།
རྣལ་འབྱོར་ངས་ཀྱང་ཉམས་ལེན་དེ་ལྟར་བགྱིས།།
ཐར་འདོད་ཁྱེད་ཀྱང་དེ་བཞིན་བསྐྱང་འཚལ་ལོ།།

དེ་ལྟར་རྒྱུ་དང་འབྲས་བུའི་ཐེག་ཆེན་གྱི།།
ལམ་མཆོག་གཉིས་ཀར་དགོས་པའི་ཐུན་མོང་ལམ།།
ཇི་བཞིན་བསྐྱེད་ནས་མཁས་པའི་དེད་དཔོན་གྱི།།
མགོན་ལ་བརྟེན་ནས་རྒྱུད་སྡེའི་རྒྱ་མཚོ་ཆེར[35]།།
ཞུགས་ནས་ཡོངས་རྫོགས་མན་ངག་བརྟེན[36]པ་དེས།།
དལ་འབྱོར་ཐོབ་པ་དོན་དང་ལྡན་པར་བྱས།།
རྣལ་འབྱོར་ངས་ཀྱང་ཉམས་ལེན་དེ་ལྟར་བགྱིས།།
ཐར་འདོད་ཁྱེད་ཀྱང་དེ་བཞིན་བསྐྱང་འཚལ་ལོ།།

རང་གི་ཡིད་ལ་གོམས་པར་བྱ་ཕྱིར་དང་།།
སྐལ་བཟང་གཞན་ལའང་ཕན་པར་བྱ་བའི་ཕྱིར།།
རྒྱལ་བ་དགྱེས་པའི་ཡོངས་སུ་རྫོགས་པའི་ལམ།།
གོ་སླའི་ངག་གིས་བཤད་པའི་དགེ་བ་དེས།།

འགྲོ་བ་ཀུན་ཀྱང་རྣམ་དག་ལམ་བཟང་དང་[༡༧]།།
འབྲལ་མེད་གྱུར་ཅིག་ཅེས་ནི་སྨོན་ལམ་འདེབས།།
རྒྱལ་འབྱོར་ངས་ཀྱང་སྨོན་ལམ་དེ་ལྟར་བཏབ།།
ཐར་འདོད་ཁྱེད་ཀྱང་དེ་བཞིན་འདེབས་འཚལ་ལོ།།

ཞེས་བྱང་ཆུབ་ལམ་གྱི་རིམ་པའི་ཉམས་ལེན་གྱི་རྣམ་གཞག་མདོར་བསྡུས་ཏེ་བརྗོད་བྱང་དུ་བྱས་པ་འདི་ནི། མང་དུ་ཐོས་པའི་དགེ་སློང་སྤོང་བ་པ་བློ་བཟང་གྲགས་པའི་དཔལ་གྱིས། འབྲོག་རི་བོ་ཆེ་དགེ་ལྡན་རྣམ་པར་རྒྱལ་བའི་གླིང་དུ་སྦྱར་བའོ།། །།

བྱང་ཆུབ་ལམ་གྱི་རིམ་པའི་ཁྲིད་བདུད་རྩི་གསེར་གྱི་ཡང་ཞུན་[1]།

རྒྱལ་བ་སྐུ་ཕྲེང་གསུམ་པ་བསོད་ནམས་རྒྱ་མཚོ།

༄༅། རྗེ་བཙུན་བླ་མ་སྐྱབས་གསུམ་ཀུན་འདུས་ཀྱི་བདག་ཉིད་ཆེན་པོ་གང་དེའི་ཞབས་ལ་གུས་པ་ཆེན་པོས་ཕྱག་འཚལ་ཞིང་སྐྱབས་སུ་མཆིའོ། །བྱིན་གྱིས་བརླབ་ཏུ་གསོལ། དེ་ལ་འདིར་དལ་འབྱོར་གྱི་རྟེན་ལ་སྙིང་པོ་ལེན་པར་འདོད་པའི་སྐྱེས་བུ་རྣམས་ཀྱིས་ཉམས་སུ་བླང་བར་བྱ་བ་ནི། རྒྱལ་བའི་གསུང་རབ་ཐམས་ཅད་ཀྱི་སྙིང་པོ། དུས་གསུམ་འཕགས་པ་ཐམས་ཅད་ཀྱི་བགྲོད་པ་གཅིག་པའི་ལམ། ཤིང་རྟ་ཆེན་པོ་ཀླུ་སྒྲུབ་དང་ཐོགས་མེད་གཉིས་ཀྱི་ལམ་སྲོལ། རྣམ་པ་ཐམས་ཅད་མཁྱེན་པའི་སར་འགྲོ་བའི་སྐྱེ་བོ་མཆོག་གི་ཆོས་ལུགས། སྐྱེས་བུ་གསུམ་གྱིས་ཉམས་སུ་བླང་བྱའི་རིམ་པ་ཐམས་ཅད་མ་ཚང་བ་མེད་པར་བསྡུས་པ། བྱང་ཆུབ་ལམ་གྱི་རིམ་པ་ཞེས་བྱ་བ་འདི་ཉིད་ཡིན་ལ།།

འདི་ལ་ཐོག་མར་ཉམས་སུ་བླང་བྱའི་ཆོས་ཁུངས་བཙུན་ཁྱད་པར་དུ་འཕགས་པ་ཞིག་ཡིན་པ་དང་། ཁུངས་བཙུན་པ་ནས་བྱུང་བའི་ཆོས་དེ་ཡང་ཕྱོགས་རེ་ཙམ་མ་ཡིན་པའི་ལམ་གྱི་ལུས་ཡོངས་སུ་རྫོགས་ཤིང་ཆ་ཚང་ལ་མ་ནོར་བ་ཞིག་དགོས་པ་ཡིན་པ་ལ། ད་རེས་བདག་གིས་ཉམས་སུ་བླང་བྱའི་ལམ་གྱི་རིམ་པ་འདི་ནི་ཡང་དག་པར་རྫོགས་པའི་སངས་རྒྱས་ནས་བཟུང་ཀླུ་སྒྲུབ་ཐོགས་མེད་གཉིས་ལས་རིམ་པ་བཞིན་བརྒྱུད་པས་ཁུངས་བཙུན་པ་ཡིན་ཞིང་། ཁུངས་བཙུན་དེ་རྣམས་ལས་བརྒྱུད་པའི་ཆོས་ཀྱི་རིམ་པ་འདིས་སྐྱེ་རྒྱུ་[2]རྣམས་ཀྱི་འདོད་དོན་མ་ལུས་པ་བདེ་བླག་ཏུ་སྐོང་བས་ན་རིན་པོ་ཆེ་དབང་

གི་རྒྱལ་པོ་ལྟ་བུ་དང་། ཐེག་པ་ཆེ་ཆུང་གི་གཞུང་ལུགས་བཟང་པོ་མ་ལུས་པའི་ལེགས་བཤད་ཀྱི་ཆུ་བོ་འདུ་བས་ན་རྒྱ་མཚོ་ཆེན་པོ་ལྟ་བུ་དང་། མདོ་སྔགས་ཀྱི་གནད་བསྡུས་ནས་སྟོན་པས་བརྗོད་བྱ་ཡོངས་སུ་རྫོགས་པ་དང་། སེམས་འདུལ་བའི་རིམ་པ་གཙོ་བོར་བྱས་པས་ཉམས་སུ་ལེན་བདེ་བ་དང་། ཀླུ་སྒྲུབ་ཀྱི་ལུགས་ལ་མཁས་པའི་རིགས་པའི་ཁྲ་བྱུག་དང་། ཐོགས་མེད་ཀྱི་ལུགས་ལ་མཁས་པའི་གསེར་གླིང་པའི་གདམས་པས་བརྒྱན་པ་ཡིན་པས་འདི་ལྟ་བུ་ལ་ཉན་བསམ་སྒོམ་གསུམ་བྱེད་དུ་ཡོད་པ་ནི་བདག་སྐལ་བ་བཟང་ལ། རང་རེའི་བླ་མའི་གསུང་མགུར་ལས་ཀྱང་། འཛམ་གླིང་མཁས་པ་ཡོངས་ཀྱི་གཙུག་གི་རྒྱན། །སྙན་པའི་བ་དན་འགྲོ་ན་ལྷང་ངེ་བ། །ཀླུ་སྒྲུབ་ཐོགས་མེད་གཉིས་ལས་རིམ་བཞིན་དུ། །ལེགས་བརྒྱུད་བྱང་ཆུབ་ལམ་གྱི་རིམ་པ་ནི། །སྐྱེ་རྒུའི་[༡]འདོད་དོན་མ་ལུས་སྐོང་བས་ན། །གདམས་པ་རིན་ཆེན་དབང་གི་རྒྱལ་པོ་སྟེ། །གཞུང་བཟང་སྟོང་གི་ཆུ་བོ་འདུ་བའི་ཕྱིར། །དཔལ་ལྡན་ལེགས་པར་བཤད་པའི་རྒྱ་མཚོའང་ཡིན། །ཞེས་གསུངས་སོ།།

དེས་ན་གདམས་པ་འདི་གཞན་ལས་ཁྱད་པར་འཕགས་པའི་ཆེ་བ་བཞི་དང་ལྡན་པ་ཡིན་ཏེ། གདམས་པ་འདི་ལ་བརྟེན་ནས་རྒྱལ་བའི་གསུང་རབ་ཇི་སྙེད་པ་ཐམས་ཅད་ལས་ཁ་ཅིག་ལམ་གྱི་གཙོ་བོ། ཁ་ཅིག་ལམ་གྱི་ཡན་ལག་སྟོན་བྱེད་དུ་ཤེས་ནས་དངོས་དང་བརྒྱུད་པ་ཅི་རིགས་པའི་སྒོ་ནས་གང་ཟག་རང་ཉིད་ལྟ་བུ་གཅིག་འཚང་རྒྱ་བའི་ཆ་རྐྱེན་དུ་གོ་བའི་བསྟན་པ་ཐམས་ཅད་འགལ་མེད་དུ་རྟོགས་པའི་ཆེ་བ།།

མདོ་སྔགས་ཀྱི་གསུང་རབ་དང་དེའི་དགོངས་འགྲེལ་གྱི་བསྟན་བཅོས་ཚད་ལྡན་རྣམས་ཕྱིའི་གོ་རྒྱ་གཅོད་པའི་བཤད་ཆོས་ཙམ་དང་། ཉམས་སུ་ལེན་རྒྱུའི་སྙིང་པོའི་ཡན་ལག་དེ་རྣམས་ལས་གཞན་ན་ཡོད་པར་འཛིན་པའི་ལོག་རྟོག་རྣམས་ལྷག་མ་མེད་པར་ལོག་ནས་གསུང་རབ་དགོངས་འགྲེལ་དང་བཅས་པའི་བརྗོད་བྱ་མཐའ་དག་བཤེས་གཉེན་བསྟེན་ཚུལ་ནས་ཞི་ལྷག་གི་བར་གྱི་ལམ་གྱི་རིམ་པར་བསྡུས་ནས་དེ་དག་གདམས་པའི་

མཐིལ་དུ་བཟུང་སྟེ་བརྗོད་བྱའི་དོན་གྱི་དཔྱད་སྒོམ་དགོས་པ་ལ་དཔྱད་སྒོམ། འཇོག་སྒོམ་དགོས་པ་ལ་འཇོག་སྒོམ་བྱེད་པའི་ཉམས་ལེན་སྟོན་པའི་གདམས་ངག་ཏུ་གོ་བར་འགྱུར་བས་ན་གསུང་རབ་ཐམས་ཅད་གདམས་ངག་ཏུ་འཆར་བའི་ཆེ་བ།།

དེ་ལྟར་གསུང་རབ་དགོངས་འགྲེལ་དང་བཅས་པའི་གཞུང་ཆེ་བ་རྣམས་གདམས་པའི་མཆོག་ཡིན་ཡང་བདག་ལྟ་བུའི་རྒྱ་ཆེན་པོའི་གསུང་རབ་ཀྱི་དོན་ལ་མ་སྦྱངས་པའི་གང་ཟག་ལས་དང་པོ་བ་རྣམས་ཀྱིས་དམ་པའི་མན་ངག་ལ་མ་བརྟེན་པར་གཞུང་ཆེན་མོ་དེ་དག་གི་དོན་ལ་ཐོས་བསམ་གྱིས་ཞུགས་ཀྱང་དགོངས་དོན་ཇི་ལྟ་བ་བཞིན་མི་རྙེད་པའམ། རྙེད་ཀྱང་དུས་རྒྱུན་རིང་ཞིང་ཚེགས་ཤིན་ཏུ་ཆེ་བ་ལ་ལྟོས་དགོས། བླ་མ་དམ་པའི་མན་ངག་ལམ་སྒྲོན་ནི་བྱང་ཆུབ་ལམ་རིམ་ཉིད་ལྟ་བུ་ལ་བརྟེན་ནས་གཞུང་ཆེན་པོ་རྣམས་ཀྱི་དོན་ཚེགས་མེད་པར་རྙེད་པས་ན་རྒྱལ་བའི་དགོངས་པ་བདེ་བླག་ཏུ་རྙེད་པའི་ཆེ་བ།།

དེ་ལྟར་རྙེད་པའི་ཚེ་སངས་རྒྱས་ཀྱི་བཀའ་ཐམས་ཅད་དངོས་དང་བརྒྱུད་པའི་སྒོ་ནས་འཚང་རྒྱ་བའི་ཐབས་སྟོན་པར་གོ་བས། འགའ་ཞིག་འཚང་རྒྱ་བའི་ཐབས་སྟོན་པར་བཟུང་ནས་སློབ་དགོས་པ་དང་། འགའ་ཞིག་འཚང་རྒྱ་བའི་གེགས་སུ་བཟུང་ནས་དོར་བྱར་བྱེད་པ་ཆོས་སྤོང་གི་ལས་ཡིན་པས། གདམས་པ་འདི་ལ་བརྟེན་ནས་སྔར་བཤད་པ་ལྟར་བསྟན་པ་ཐམས་ཅད་འགལ་མེད་དུ་རྟོགས་པའི་ངེས་པ་རྙེད་པ་ཙམ་གྱིས་དེ་ལྟ་བུའི་ཆོས་སྤོང་གི་ཉེས་སྤྱོད་ཆེན་པོ་རང་འགགས་སུ་འགྱུར་བའི་ཆེ་བ་རྣམས་དང་ལྡན་པའི་ཕྱིར།།

དེ་ལྟར་ན་གསུང་རབ་ཀྱི་དོན་ལ་དཔྱོད་པའི་རྣམ་དཔྱོད་དང་ལྡན་པའམ། ལྡན་པར་འདོད་ན་ནི་རྒྱ་བོད་ཀྱི་མཁས་པའི་སྐྱེ་བོ་སྐལ་ལྡན་དུ་མས་བརྟེན་ཅིང་ཐུགས་ཉམས་སུ་བཞེས་པའི་གདམས་པ་མཆོག་ཏུ་གྱུར་པ་སྐྱེས་བུ་གསུམ་གྱི་ལམ་གྱི་རིམ་པ་འདིས་

ཡིད་རང་དབང་མེད་པར་ཕྲོགས་ཏེ་ཉན་བསམ་སྒོམ་པ་ལ་འཇུག་རིགས་ཏེ། གདམས་པ་དེ་ཉིད་གོང་དུ་བཤད་པ་ལྟར་གྱི་ཆེ་བ་བཞི་དང་ལྡན་པས་སོ། རྗེ་བླ་མས་ཀྱང་། བསྟན་པ་ཐམས་ཅད་འགལ་མེད་རྟོགས་པ་དང་། །གསུང་རབ་མ་ལུས་གདམས་པར་འཆར་བ་དང་། །རྒྱལ་བའི་དགོངས་པ་བདེ་བླག་རྙེད་པ་དང་། །ཉེས་སྤྱོད་ཆེན་པོའི་གཡང་ས་ལས་ཀྱང་སྲུང༌། །དེ་ཕྱིར་རྒྱ་བོད་མཁས་པའི་སྐྱེ་བོ་ནི། །སྐལ་ལྡན་དུ་མས་བསྟེན་པའི་གདམས་པ་མཆོག །སྐྱེས་བུ་གསུམ་གྱི་ལམ་གྱི་རིམ་པ་ཡིས། །ཡིད་རབ་མི་འཕྲོག་དཔྱོད་ལྡན་སུ་ཞིག་ཡོད། །ཅེས་གསུངས་པས་སོ།།

དེ་ལྟ་བུའི་ཆེ་བ་དང་ལྡན་པའི་གདམས་པ་རྒྱལ་བའི་གསུང་རབ་ཀུན་གྱི་སྙིང་པོ་ཕྱོགས་གཅིག་ཏུ་བསྡུས་པ་སྐྱེས་བུ་གསུམ་གྱི་ལམ་གྱི་རིམ་པའི་ཚུལ་འདི་ཡོངས་སུ་རྫོགས་པ་ལྟ་ཅི་སྨོས། ཐུན་རེ་ཙམ་སྟོན་ཚུལ་ཕྱིན་ཅི་མ་ལོག་པར་སྟོན་ཅིང་བཤད་པའི་ཕན་ཡོན་བསམས་ཏེ། སྟོན་པ་དང་ཆོས་ལ་རིམ་གྲོ་བསྐྱེད། བསམ་སྦྱོར་རྣམ་དག་གི་སྒོ་ནས་སྟོད་ལྡན་གྱི་གང་ཟག་ལ་ཕྱིན་ཅི་མ་ལོག་པར་སྟོན་པ་ལས་དམ་ཆོས་ཚུལ་བཞིན་བཤད་པའི་ཕན་ཡོན་རླབས་ཆེན་པོ་སྡུད་པ་དང་། ཉན་ཚུལ་ཕྱིན་ཅི་མ་ལོག་པར་སྟོད་ཀྱི་སྐྱོན་གསུམ་སྤང་བ་དང་འདུ་ཤེས་དྲུག་བསྟེན་པ་སོགས་ཀྱི་སྒོ་ནས་ཉན་པ་ལ་དམ་ཆོས་ཐོས་པའི་ཕན་ཡོན་རླབས་ཆེན་སྡུད་པ་དེ་འབྱུང་བར་ངེས་པས། ཉན་བཤད་ཚུལ་བཞིན་དུ་བྱེད་པ་ལ་འབད་པར་བྱ་རིགས་ཤིང་བྱེད་དགོས་ཏེ། རྗེ་བླ་མས། གསུང་རབ་ཀུན་གྱི་སྙིང་པོ་བསྡུ་བསྡུ་བ། །ཚུལ་འདི་ཐུན་རེ་སྟོན་དང་ཉན་པས་ཀྱང་། །དམ་ཆོས་འཆད་དང་ཐོས་པའི་ཕན་ཡོན་ཚོགས། །རླབས་ཆེན་སྡུད་པར་ངེས་པས་དེ་དོན་བསམ། །ཞེས་གསུངས་པས་སོ།།

འོ་ན་དེ་ལྟ་བུའི་གདམས་པ་ཚུལ་བཞིན་དུ་ཉན་པ་ལ་ཕན་ཡོན་རླབས་ཆེན་འབྱུང་བ་དེ་ལྟ་ན། གདམས་པ་ཁྱད་པར་ཅན་དེ་གང་ཟག་ཇི་ལྟ་བུ་ཞིག་ལས་ཉན་དགོས་སྙམ

ན། སྤྱིར་དམ་པའི་ཆོས་ཉན་པར་འོས་པའི་བཤེས་གཉེན་ལ་ཐེག་པ་ཆེ་ཆུང་དང་མདོ་སྔགས་ཀྱི་སྐབས་ལས་བཤེས་གཉེན་གྱི་མཚན་ཉིད་མི་འདྲ་བ་མང་དུ་གསུངས་ཀྱང་། གདམས་པ་རིན་པོ་ཆེ་འདི་ལྟ་བུའི་བཀའ་དྲིན་ཆོད་པའི་དགེ་བའི་བཤེས་གཉེན་ནི་མདོ་སྡེ་རྒྱན་ལས་བཤད་པ་ལྟར་ལ། དུལ་བ་ཚུལ་ཁྲིམས་ཀྱི་བསླབ་པ། ཞི་བ་ཏིང་ངེ་འཛིན་གྱི་བསླབ་པ། ཉེ་བར་ཞི་བ་ཤེས་རབ་ཀྱི་བསླབ་པ་སྟེ་བསླབ་པ་གསུམ་གྱི་སྒོ་ནས་རྒྱུད་དུལ་བར་བྱས་པའི་རྟོགས་པའི་ཡོན་ཏན་དང་། སྡེ་སྣོད་གསུམ་ལ་སོགས་པ་མང་དུ་ཐོས་པ་ལུང་གི་ཡོན་ཏན་དང་། དེ་ཁོ་ན་ཉིད་རབ་ཏུ་རྟོགས་པའི་ཤེས་རབ་དང་ལྡན་པ། སློབ་མ་ལས་ཡོན་ཏན་ལྷག་པ་སྟེ་ཆོས་སྨྲ་བ་པོ་རང་གིས་ཐོབ་པའི་ཡོན་ཏན་དྲུག་དང་། ལམ་ལ་ཇི་ལྟར་བགྲོ་བའི་རིམ་པ་ལ་མཁས་ཤིང་དོན་གདུལ་བྱའི་རྣ་བར་སྐྱོལ་བའི་སྨྲ་མཁས་པ། རྙེད་བཀུར་སོགས་ལ་མི་ལྟ་བར་སྙིང་རྗེས་ཀུན་ནས་བསླང་སྟེ་ཆོས་སྟོན་པས་ཀུན་སློང་དག་པ་བརྩེ་བ་དང་། ཆོས་བཤད་པ་སོགས་ཀྱི་གཞན་དོན་ལ་སྤྲོ་བའི་བརྩོན་པ་དང་བཅས་པ་དང་། འཆད་པའི་དཀའ་སྤྱད་དང་། འཁོར་གྱིས་ལོག་སྒྲུབ་མི་བཟོད་པའི་རྟོག་པ་སྤངས་པ་སྟེ་གཞན་རྗེས་སུ་འཛིན་པའི་ཡོན་ཏན་བཞི་དང་ལྡན་པ་སྟེ་ཆོས་བཅུ་ལྡན་ཞིག་བསྟེན་ནས་ཐེག་ཆེན་གྱི་གདམས་པ་དང་རྗེས་སུ་བསྟན་པ་ཉན་པར་བྱ་ཞིང་།།

ཉན་པ་པོའི་གང་ཟག་ཀྱང་སྤྱིར་གཟུ་བོར་གནས་པ། ལམ་ཡང་དག་པ་དང་ལྟར་སྣང་གི་རྣམ་དབྱེ་འབྱེད་པའི་བློ་དང་ལྡན་པ། ལམ་ཡང་དག་དོན་དུ་གཉེར་བ་གསུམ། དེའི་སྟེང་དུ་ཆོས་དང་ཆོས་སྨྲ་བ་ལ་གུས་པ་སྟེ་བཞི་ལྡན་དགོས་ལ། ཁྱད་པར་ལམ་འདི་ལྟ་བུ་ལ་བགྲོར་རུང་བའི་སློབ་མ་མཚན་ཉིད་དང་ལྡན་པ་ལ་ཆོས་ལ་དོན་གཉེར་ཆེ་བ། ཉན་པའི་ཚེ་ཡིད་ལེགས་པར་གཏོད་པ། ཆོས་དང་ཆོས་སྨྲ་བ་ལ་དད་གུས་ཆེ་བ། ཉེས་བཤད་དོར་ནས་ལེགས་བཤད་འཛིན་པའི་ཆོས་བཞི་ལྡན་དང་། དེའི་མཐུན་རྐྱེན་བློ་དང་ལྡན་པ། འགལ་རྐྱེན་འདོར་བ་གཟུར་གནས་ཏེ་དྲུག་ལྡན་དུ་བྱ་དགོས་པས་རང་ཡང་

ལམ་འདི་སྟོན་པ་པོ་བྱེད་འདོད་ན་བཤེས་གཉེན་གྱི་མཚན་ཉིད་དེ་དག་ལྡན་པ་[༥]ལ་འབད། ཉན་པའི་ཚེ་ཉན་པ་པོའི་མཚན་ཉིད་དང་ལྡན་པ་ལ་བསླབ་བོ།།

དགེ་བའི་བཤེས་གཉེན་མཚན་ཉིད་དང་ལྡན་པ་ཞིག་ལས་གདམས་ངག་སྐྱེས་བུ་གསུམ་གྱི་ལམ་གྱི་རིམ་པ་ཚུལ་བཞིན་ཉན་ནས་ཉམས་སུ་ཇི་ལྟར་ལེན་པའི་ཚུལ་ནི། དང་པོར་གནས་ཡིད་དང་མཐུན་པར་དཀོན་མཆོག་གི་རྟེན་བཀྲམ། མཆོད་པ་གཡོ་མེད་པར་ལེགས་པར་བཤམས། སྟན་བདེ་བ་ལ་སྐྱིལ་ཀྲུང་བཅས། བསམ་པ་ཐག་པ་ནས་བློ་ཧྲོས་བཀལ་པའི་[༦]སྐྱབས་འགྲོ་རྒྱུད་དང་འདྲེས་པ་མང་དུ་བྱས། ཚད་མེད་པ་བཞི་བསྒོམས། སངས་རྒྱས་ཆོས་དང་ཚོགས་ཀྱི་མཆོག་རྣམས་ལ། ཞེས་སོགས་ཀྱིས་སེམས་བསྐྱེད། ཨོཾ་སྭ་བྷཱ་ཝས་ཆོས་ཐམས་ཅད་རང་བཞིན་གྱིས་གྲུབ་པས་སྟོང་པའི་སྟོང་པ་ཉིད་དུ་གྱུར། སྟོང་པའི་ངང་ལས་མདུན་གྱི་ནམ་མཁར་སེང་གེ་ཆེན་པོ་བརྒྱད་ཀྱིས་བཏེག[༧](བཏེགས་)པའི་རིན་པོ་ཆེའི་ཁྲི་ཡངས་ཤིང་རྒྱ་ཆེ་བའི་སྟེང་དུ་སྣ་ཚོགས་པདྨ་དང་ཟླ་བའི་གདན་གྱི་སྟེང་དུ་རང་ལ་ལམ་འདི་སྟོན་པའི་བླ་མ་དང་དབྱེར་མེད་པའི་བདག་ཅག་གི་སྟོན་པ་ལ་རྒྱ་ཆེན་སྤྱོད་བརྒྱུད་དང་ཟབ་མོ་ལྟ་བརྒྱུད་ཀྱི་བླ་མས་བསྐོར་བ་དང་། དེའི་མཐར་ཕྱོགས་བཅུའི་སངས་རྒྱས་བྱང་སེམས་ཉན་ཐོས་རང་རྒྱལ། དཔའ་བོ་མཁའ་འགྲོ་བཀའ་སྲུང་རྒྱ་མཚོའི་ཚོགས་ཀྱིས་བསྐོར་བ་སྤྱན་དྲངས་ནས་བཞུགས་པར་གྱུར། རྣམ་དག་ཆོས་ཀྱི་དབྱིངས་ལས་མ་གཡོས་ཀྱང་། །ཐུགས་རྗེས་ཚད་མེད་འགྲོ་ལ་ཕྱོགས་བཅུར་གཟིགས། །རྒྱལ་བ་ཀུན་གྱི་འཕྲིན་ལས་རྒྱས་མཛད་པའི། །དུས་གསུམ་བླ་མ་འཁོར་བཅས་གཤེགས་སུ་གསོལ། །མ་ལུས་སེམས་ཅན་ཀུན་གྱི་མགོན་གྱུར་ཅིང་། །ཞེས་སོགས་ཀྱིས་སྤྱན་དྲངས།།

ཁྲུས་ཀྱི་ཁང་པ་ཤིན་ཏུ་དྲི་ཞིམ་པ། ཞེས་སོགས་ཀྱིས་ཁྲུས་ཁང་བསྐྱེད་པ། ཁྲུས་

གསོལ་བ། སྐུ་དབྱེ་བ། ན་བཟའ་དང་རྒྱན་འབུལ་བ། བདག་དང་འགྲོ་ལ། སོགས་ཀྱིས་མཆོད་པ། ཚོགས་ཀྱི་ཞིང་དུ་བཞུགས་སུ་གསོལ་བ་རྣམས་སྒྲིད་འཇུག་ནས་འབྱུང་བ་ལྟར་བྱ། དེ་ནས་བསག་སྦྱང་གི་གནད་བསྡུས་པ་ཡན་ལག་བདུན་[༡] (པ་) བྱ་བ་ནི། ཐོག་མར། སངས་རྒྱས་ཐམས་ཅད་འདུས་པའི་སྐུ། ཞེས་སོགས་དང་། ཐུགས་རྗེ་ཆེན་པོ་བདེ་གཤེགས་རྡོ་རྗེ་འཆང་། །ཆོས་གཟིགས་ཧེ་ལོ་པ་དང་། ཞེས་སོགས་ཀྱིས་ཉམས་ལེན་བྱིན་རླབས་བརྒྱུད་དང་། བྱམས་པ་ཐོགས་མེད་དབྱིག་གཉེན་རྣམ་གྲོལ་སྡེ། ཞེས་སོགས་ཀྱིས་རྒྱ་ཆེན་སྤྱོད་བརྒྱུད་དང་། ཡོད་མེད་ཕྱོགས་འཛིག་རྒྱལ་སྲས་ཀླུ་སྒྲུབ་དང་། ཞེས་སོགས་ཀྱིས་ཟབ་མོ་ལྟ་བརྒྱུད། རྒྱལ་བའི་མདུན་ན། ཞེས་སོགས་ཀྱི་ཇོ་བོ་། ཡོངས་ཀྱི་དགེ་བའི་བཤེས་གཉེན། ཞེས་སོགས་ཀྱིས་འབྲོམ་། དམིགས་མེད་བརྩེ་བའི་གཏེར་ཆེན་སྤྱན་རས་གཟིགས། ཞེས་སོགས་ཀྱི་རྗེ་དང་། ལུང་རིགས་སོགས་འདྲ། རླབས་ཆེན་ཤེས་རབ་ཟབ་མོའི་ལུས་སྟོབས་རྒྱས། ཞེས་སོགས་དང་། རིག་གྲོལ་ཕུན་ཚོགས་ཞེས་སོགས་དང་། དགོས་འདོད་ཀུན་འབྱུང་། ཞེས་སོགས་དང་། གང་ལ་བདག་ཅག་རིག་པ་བསླབས་པ་དང་། ཞེས་སོགས་དང་། སྟོན་པ་བླ་མེད་སངས་རྒྱས་རིན་པོ་ཆེ། ཞེས་སོགས་དང་། ཐབས་མཁས་ཐུགས་རྗེས་ཤཱཀྱའི་རིགས་སུ་འཁྲུངས། ཞེས་སོགས་དང་། ཇི་སྙེད་སུ་དག་ཅེས་པ་ནས། ཕྱག་འཚལ་མཆོད་པར་བགྱི། ཞེས་པའི་བར་བྱས། དེ་ནས་མཎྜལ་རྒྱས་བསྡུས་གང་ཡང་རུང་བ་དང་། དེ་ལས་གཞན་ཡང་མཆོད་པའི་ཚོགས། ཞེས་པ་ནས། སྲིན་རྣམས་སོ་སོར་གནས་གྱུར་ཅིག ཅེས་པའི་བར་དང་། སྐྱེ་བཤགས་ཚར་གསུམ་བྱས། འདོད་ཆགས་ཞེ་སྡང་གཏི་མུག་དབང་གིས་ནི། ཞེས་པ་ནས། བྱང་ཆུབ་ཕྱིར་བསྔོའོ། ཞེས་པའི་བར་བྱ། དེ་ནས་ལམ་རིམ་གསོལ་འདེབས་ལམ་མཆོག་སྒོ་འབྱེད་གདངས་ཡིད་འཕྲུལ་བ་དང་བཅས་ཏེ་གདོན། དེ་

ནས་མཆོད་ཡུལ་རྣམས་རང་བཞིན་གྱི་གནས་སུ་གཤེགས་ཞེས་གཤེགས་གསོལ་བྱ། བྱུན་བཞི་འམ་བྱུན་དྲུག་ཏུ་ཉམས་སུ་ལེན་ན་བྱུན་ཐ་མ་ལ་གཤེགས་གསོལ་བྱ། དེ་ནི་བཤེས་གཉེན་བསྟེན་ཚུལ་གྱི་སྔོན་འགྲོའོ།།

བསྟེན་ཚུལ་དངོས་ནི་དཔྱད་སྒོམ་གྱི་སྒོ་ནས་བསྒོམ་པར་བྱ་སྟེ། དེ་ཡང་བདག་གི་དཔལ་ལྡན་བླ་མ་དམ་པ་འདི་རྣམས་དངོས་གྲུབ་ཐམས་ཅད་ཀྱི་རྩ་བ། འདི་ཕྱིའི་ལེགས་ཚོགས་ཐམས་ཅད་ཀྱི་འབྱུང་གནས་ཡིན། སྨན་པ་དང་ནད་པ་བཞིན་དུ་བླ་མས་སྡུག་བསྔལ་གྱི་ནད་སེལ་བས་སྐུ་དྲིན་ཆེ། འཁོར་བ་ཐོག་མ་མེད་པ་ནས་ད་བར་འཁོར་བར་གཏན་འཁྲུམས་བྱས་པ་འདི་བཤེས་གཉེན་དམ་པ་དེ་དང་མ་མཇལ་བའམ། མཇལ་ཀྱང་དེའི་བཀའ་བཞིན་མ་བསྒྲུབས་པས་ལན། ད་ནི་ངས་བླ་མ་ཅི་མཉེས་བྱེད་དགོས། ཟས་ནོར་འབྲངས་ནས་སྐྱིད་རྒྱགས་པའི་སྐབས་སུ་གསེར་སྲྨ་ལག་པས་ཐེག་ཚད་བྱིན་པ་ལས་ལྟོགས་དྲི་ལ་འཆི་ལ་ཁད་ལ་ཟས་ཕོར་གང་སྟེར་བ་དྲིན་ཆེ་བ་བཞིན། ང་ལ་ནི་རིམ་“ལྷ་ལས་[༡༠]། འདི་ནི་རང་བྱུང་བཅོམ་ལྡན་འདས། །ལྷག་པའི་ལྷ་ནི་གཅིག་པུ་ཉིད། །མན་ངག་རབ་ཏུ་སྟེར་བའི་ཕྱིར། །རྡོ་རྗེ་སློབ་དཔོན་དེ་བས་ལྷག །ཅེས་གསུངས་པ་ལྟར་སངས་རྒྱས་རྣམས་ལས་ཀྱང་བླ་མ་འདི་བཀའ་དྲིན་ཆེ་ངེས་བསམ།།

སྔོན་བདག་ཅག་གི་སྟོན་པས། སྐྱེ་བ་ཡོད་ན་འཆི་བ་ཡོད། །འགོག་པ་འདི་ནི་བདེ་བ་ཡིན། །ཞེས་པའི་ཚིགས་བཅད་ཕྱེད་ཙམ་དང་། ཚིགས་བཅད་རེ་ཙམ་གསན་པའི་བླ་མ་ལ་བཀའ་དྲིན་བསམས་པའམ་བླ་མ་དེ་མཉེས་པར་བྱ་བའི་ཕྱིར་གསེར་སྲང་འབུམ་ཕྲག་ཕུལ་བ་དང་། རྒྱལ་པོའི་སྲས་དང་བཙུན་མོ་ལ་སོགས་པ་ཆེས་ཕངས་པ་ཕུལ་བ། སྐུ་ལུས་ལ་མར་མེ་སྟོང་བཙུགས་པ་སོགས་ལུས་ལོངས་སྤྱོད་ཐམས་ཅད་གཏོང་བར་མཛད་འདུག །བདག་ཀྱང་སྟོན་པ་དེའི་རྗེས་འཇུག་ཡིན་ཞིང་། ད་ལྟའི་བླ་མ་རྣམས

ལ་ཆོས་ཚད་མེད་པ་ཉན་ཡོད་པས་བཀའ་དྲིན་ཚད་མེད་ཨང་། གལ་ཏེ་ད་ལྟའི་བླ་མ་སྐུ་ཡོན་ཆེ་བ་ཡིན་ན་བཀའ་དྲིན་རེ་ཙམ་འཁྱུར། དེ་མིན་ཅིར་ཡང་མི་རྩི་བའི་ཁར། ངས་ཆོས་ཉན་ཡོད་ཟེར་ཕར་དགྲེན་[༡༡]པ་བྱེད་པར་འདུག་སྟེ། དེ་ནི་མ་གོ་བ་ཤིན་ཏུ་ཆེ་བ་ཡིན་ཏེ། དཔེར་ན་ཕམ་ལ་ཡོན་ཏན་མེད་ཀྱང་དྲིན་ལེགས་པར་འཁྱུར་དགོས་ཤིང་། ཁྱུར་ན་ཕན་ཡོན་དང་། མ་ཁྱུར་ན་ཉེས་དམིགས་ཆེ་བ་བཞིན་དུ་བླ་མ་ལའང་མཚུངས་པ་ཡིན་ནོ།།

ད་ལྟ་ནོར་ཙུང་ཟད་རེ་བྱིན་པ་ལ་ཡང་དྲིན་ཆེ་ཟེར་ན། བླ་མས་ཚེ་འདི་ཕྱི་ཐམས་ཅད་ཀྱི་བདེ་བ་ལ་སྦྱོར་བ་ཡིན། ལེགས་པར་བརྟགས་ན་ཡ་གི་སངས་རྒྱས་བྱང་སེམས་ནས་ཁྲིམ་པ་རྣམས་ཀྱི་བར་ཐམས་ཅད་ལ་བླ་མ་མཉེས་པར་བྱས་མ་བྱས་ཀྱིས་སྐྱིད་སྡུག་གི་ཁྱད་པར་མངོན་དུ་མཐོང་བ་དང་། དེ་ར་མ་ཟད་བླ་མས་ཚེ་གཅིག་ལ་སངས་རྒྱས་ལ་བཀོད་པ་ཡང་མང་དུ་བྱུང་། ངས་ཀྱང་བླ་མ་རྣམས་མཆོད་པ་གསུམ་གྱིས་མཉེས་པར་བྱས་ན་སངས་རྒྱས་མྱུར་དུ་འཐོབ་ངེས། དེས་ན་བླ་མའི་བཀའ་དྲིན་ནི་བསམ་གྱིས་མི་ཁྱབ་པས་བཀའ་དྲིན་ཅན་གྱི་བླ་མ་མཉེས་པ་གལ་ཆེ་སྟེ། ཚེ་ཕྱི་མ་རྣམས་སུ་བཤེས་གཉེན་དམ་པ་དང་མཇལ་ཞིང་རྗེས་སུ་འཛིན་པ་ཡང་ད་ལྟ་ཆོས་འབྲེལ་ཡོད་པའི་བླ་མ་རྣམས་མཉེས་པར་བྱེད་པ་ཁོ་ན་ལ་རག་ལས་པས་བཤེས་གཉེན་བསྟེན་ཚུལ་མ་འཆུགས་པ་ཅིག་[༡༢]མི་བྱེད་པའི་ཐབས་རང་མི་འདུག་ཨང་།།

མདོ་བསྟན་བཅོས་ཐམས་ཅད་ལས་ཀྱང་། བླ་མ་རྣམས་མཉེས་པ་སྒྲུབ་ཤིག་ཅེས་ཡང་ཡང་གསུངས་ཤིང་། དེ་ངེད་རང་ལ་མི་འདོད་གདམ་ཁའམ་[༡༣]ཁྲོད་བཀལ་བ་ནི་མིན། བསོད་ནམས་མི་འདོད་པ་ནི་སུ་ཡང་མེད། བསོད་ནམས་གསོག་པའི་ཞིང་ནི་བླ་མ་ལས་ལྷག་པ་མེད་པར་མདོ་རྒྱུད་བསྟན་བཅོས་ཀུན་ནས་གསུངས། མཉེས་པ་སྒྲུབ་པའང་བླ་མ་ལ་སྐྱོན་རྟོག་གི་བློ་ཡི་མ་ཤོར་བའི་ཅི་མཛད་ལེགས་པར་ལྟ་བའི་སྣོ་ནས་

དད་པ་ཁ་ཙམ་མིན་པར་སྙིང་ཁོང་རུས་པའི་དཀྱིལ་ནས་བསྒོམ་སྟེ། མཚན་ཐོས་པའམ་བླ་མ་དེ་དྲན་པ་ཙམ་གྱིས་ལུས་ཀྱི་བ་སྤུ་གཡོ། མིག་ནས་མཆི་མ་འཛག་པ་སོགས་མ་བྱུང་གི་བར་དུ་བསྒོམ། དེ་ཡང་སྤྱིར་སེམས་ཅན་གང་གི་སྐྱོན་ལ་ཡང་རྟོག་ཏུ་མི་རུང་བར་རྒྱལ་བ་སྲས་བཅས་ཀྱིས་གསུངས་ན་བླ་མ་ལ་ལྟ་ཅི་སྨོས། སྐྱོན་ཡོད་པ་ལྟར་སྣང་ཡང་ང་རང་སྣང་བ་མ་དག་པ་ཡིན། བླ་མ་ལ་དེ་ལྟ་བུའི་སྐྱོན་ག་ལ་མངའ།།

སྔོན་འཕགས་པ་ཐོགས་མེད་ཀྱིས་བྱམས་པ་བསྒྲུབས་པས་ཁྱི་མོ་སྨད་ཁོག་འབུས་གང་བར་གཟིགས་པ་དང་། ནཱ་རོ་པས་ཏི་ལོ་པ་ཉ་གསོལ་ཕྱག་ཕྱེད་ཡར་གཟིགས་པ་སོགས་དང་། ཡབ་སྲས་མཇལ་བའི་མདོ་སོགས་ལས་སངས་རྒྱས་ཀྱིས་བདུད་[14]སྤྲུལ་ནས་སེམས་ཅན་གྱི་དོན་མཛད་པར་ཡང་བཤད། དེས་ན་བླ་མ་ལ་སྐྱོན་ག་ལ་ཡོད[15]། སངས་རྒྱས་དངོས་ཡིན་ངེས་སྙམ་དུ་བསམ། དེ་ལྟ་མིན་པར་བླ་མ་ལ་སྐྱོན་རྟོག་གི་སྒོ་ནས་བརྙས་སྨོད་སོགས་བྱས་ན་ནི་གསང་འདུས་རྩ་རྒྱུད་དང་བླ་མ་ལྔ་བཅུ་པ་སོགས་ལས་སྡིག་པ་གང་ལས་ཆེས་ཆེ་བའི་སྡིག་པར་བཤད་ཡོད། དེས་ན་བདག་གིས་འབྲོམ་སྟོན་པའི་རྣམ་ཐར་ལྟར་བླ་མ་མང་པོ་ཚམ་ཚོམ་དུ་མི་འཚོལ། གང་ལ་བླ་མ་བཅོལ་བ་དེ་སྲོག་དང་བསྡོས་ནས་མ་གུས་པའི་བསམ་པ་གཏན་མ་སྐྱེས་པར་བྱེད་དགོས་ཨང་སྙམ་དུ་བསྒོམ་མོ། །རྗེ་བླ་མས་ཀྱང་། དེ་ནས་འདི་ཕྱིའི་ལེགས་ཚོགས་ཇི་སྙེད་པའི། །རྟེན་འབྲེལ་ལེགས་པར་འགྲིག་པའི་རྩ་བ་ནི། །ལམ་སྟོན་བཤེས་གཉེན་དམ་པ་འབད་པ་ཡིས། །བསམ་དང་སྦྱོར་བས་ཚུལ་བཞིན་བསྟེན་པ་རུ། །མཐོང་ནས་སྲོག་གི་ཕྱིར་ཡང་མི་གཏོང་བར། །བཀའ་བཞིན་སྒྲུབ་[16]པའི་མཆོད་པས་མཉེས་པར་བྱ། །རྣལ་འབྱོར་ངས་ཀྱང་ཉམས་ལེན་དེ་ལྟར་བྱས[17]། །ཐར་འདོད་ཁྱེད་ཀྱང་དེ་བཞིན་བསྐྱང་འཚལ་ལོ། །ཞེས་བཙུན་པ་ཆེན་པོས་གདམས་པ་མཛད་དོ།།

འོ་ན་ལམ་སྟོན་པའི་བཤེས་གཉེན་དེ་ལྟར་འབད་པས་བསྟེན་ཅིང་བཀའ་བཞིན་སྒྲུབ་པའི་མཆོད་པས་མཉེས་པར་བྱ་དགོས་ན་བཀའ་ཇི་ལྟ་བུ་བསྒྲུབ་སྙམ་ན། བཤེས་གཉེན་དེས་ཇི་ལྟར་གདམས་པའི་དམ་པའི་ཆོས་ལུགས་བཞིན་དུ་ཉམས་སུ་བླངས་ཏེ། རྒྱུ་དང་འབྲས་བུའི་སྒོ་ནས་ཤིན་ཏུ་རྙེད་དཀའ་ཞིང་རྙེད་ན་དོན་ཆེ་བའི་དལ་འབྱོར་ཡིད་བཞིན་གྱི་ནོར་བུ་ལས་ལྷག་པ་འདི་དོན་ལྡན་དུ་བྱེད་པ་ལས་ལྷག་པའི་བཀའ་བཞིན་སྒྲུབ་པའི་མཆོད་པ་གཞན་མི་འདུག་པས་དེས་ན་ངས་མ་ལོ་སོར་གསུམ་ཁར་བཅུག་ནས་མི་ལུས་ལན་གཅིག་ཐོབ་པ་འདི་སྟོང་ལོག་ཏུ་མ་སོང་བ་ཞིག་མ་བྱས་ན་ངའི་སྙིང་རུ་ལ་བ་དང་འདྲ། ཚེ་འདིའི་དགྲ་འདུལ་གཉེན་སྐྱོང་གཞན་ངོར་གྲུབ་པ་ཞིག་དང་། རྙེད་བཀུར་སོགས་དོན་གཉེར་གྱི་བསམ་པས་ཀུན་ནས་བསླང་བའི་ཆོས་འཆད་ཉན། བསླབ་པའི་སྤྱང་སྡོམ་སོགས་ཆོས་བརྒྱད་དཀར་ནག་ཁྲ་གསུམ་པོ་འདི་བཙན་ཆོད་དུ་བཞག་ནས་མི་རྟག་པ་སྒོམ་པ་སོགས་ཀྱི་ཁ་ཞེ་མཐུན་ངེས་ཀྱི་ཆོས་ཤིག་ཉམས་སུ་མ་བླངས་ན་མདུན་མ་ཉེས་ཚབས་གཞན་ལས་ཆེ། རྟེན་འདི་ལ་རང་གིས་རང་ལ་མི་ཁྲེལ་བའི་ཆོས་རྣམ་དག་ཅིག་ཉམས་སུ་བླངས་ན་ནི་ནམ་གཞག་ (ཞག་) གཏན་གྱི་མདུན་མའི་རྐང་ཚུགས་ཏེ་ལེགས་ཚབས་གཞན་ལས་ཆེ་བ་འདུག །དེས་ན་ངས་ཁེ་ཆུང་ལ་ཉེན་ཆེ་བའི་འཇིག་རྟེན་གྱི་བྱ་བ་སྙིང་པོ་མེད་པའི་སྤྱུན་པ་[༡༨](སྤྲུན་)ཕྱུར་བ་འདི་ལས་ལོག[༡༩] །མི་ལུས་འདི་དོན་ལྡན་འཆི་ཁར་འགྱོད་མི་དགོས་པ་སྙིང་པོ་ཡོད་པ་ཞིག་བྱེད། དེ་ཡང་ད་ལྟ་ཉིད་དུ་བྱེད་སྙམ་པའི་སྒོ་ནས་དལ་འབྱོར་ལ་སྙིང་པོ་ལེན་འདོད་སྐྱེམ་པས་གདུངས་པ་ཆུ་དོན་དུ་གཉེར་བ་ལྟར་བསྒོམ་པར་བྱ་ཞིང་། རྗེ་བླ་མས་ཀྱང་། དལ་བའི་རྟེན་འདི་ཡིད་བཞིན་ནོར་ལས་ལྷག །འདི་འདྲ་རྙེད་པ་ད་རེས་ཙམ་ཞིག་ཡིན། །རྙེད་དཀའ་འཇིག་སླ་ནམ་མཁའི་གློག་དང་འདྲ། །ཚུལ་འདི་བསམས་ནས་འཇིག་རྟེན་བྱ་བ་ཀུན།

།སྤྱིན་[༣༠]（སྦྱིན་）པ་འཕྱུར་བ་བཞིན་དུ་རྫོགས་གྱུར་ནས། །ཉིན་མཚན་ཀུན་ཏུ་སྙིང་པོ་ལེན་པ་དགོས། །ཞེས་ཀྱང་གསུངས་ཡོད་ཨང་སྐམ་དུ་བསམ།།

འོ་ན་དལ་འབྱོར་གྱི་རྟེན་ལ་སྙིང་པོ་ལེན་དགོས་ན། སྙིང་པོ་ཇི་ལྟར་ལེན་དགོས་སྐམ་ན་འདི་ལ་གཉིས་གསུངས་པའི། དང་པོ་ལམ་སྤྱིའི་རྣམ་གཞག་ལ་ངེས་པ་སྐྱེད་ཚུལ་འདི་ལ་གོ་བ་ཆགས་པ་ཤིན་ཏུ་གལ་ཆེ་བས་ཅུང་ཟད་བཤད་ན་འདི་ལ་གཉིས། སྐྱེས་བུ་གསུམ་གྱི་ལམ་དུ་གསུང་རབ་ཐམས་ཅད་འདུས་པའི་ཚུལ། སྐྱེས་བུ་གསུམ་གྱི་སྒོ་ནས་འཁྲིད་པའི་རྒྱུ་མཚན་བསྟན་པའོ།།

དང་པོ་ནི། སངས་རྒྱས་དང་པོར་ཐུགས་བསྐྱེད། བར་དུ་ཚོགས་བསགས། ཐ་མར་སངས་རྒྱས་པ་ཐམས་ཅད་སེམས་ཅན་གྱི་དོན། ཆོས་གསུངས་པ་ཐམས་ཅད་ཀྱང་སེམས་ཅན་གྱི་དོན་ཁོ་ན་ཡིན་ལ། བསྒྲུབ་བྱ་སེམས་ཅན་གྱི་དོན་ལ་གནས་སྐབས་མངོན་མཐོ་དང་མཐར་ཐུག་ངེས་ལེགས་གཉིས་ལས་དང་པོ་སྒྲུབ་ཚུལ་ལས་བརྩམས་ཏེ་གསུངས་པ་ཐམས་ཅད་སྐྱེས་བུ་ཆུང་ངུ་དངོས་སམ་ཆུང་ངུ་དང་ཐུན་མོང་བའི་ཆོས་སྐོར་དུ་འདུ་སྟེ། སྐྱེས་བུ་ཆུང་ངུའི་ཁྱད་པར་ནི་ལམ་སྒྲོན་ལས། གང་ཞིག་ཐབས་ནི་གང་དག་གིས། །འཁོར་བའི་བདེ་བ་ཙམ་དག་ལ། །རང་ཉིད་དོན་དུ་གཉེར་བྱེད་པ། །དེ་ནི་སྐྱེས་བུ་ཐ་མར་ཤེས། །ཞེས་གསུངས་པ་ལྟར་ཚེ་འདི་ལ་ཆེད་ཆེར་མི་བྱེད་པར་ཕྱི་མར་མཐོ་རིས་ཀྱི་བདེ་བ་དོན་དུ་གཉེར་ཞིང་དེའི་རྒྱུ་ཉམས་སུ་ལེན་པ་ཞིག་ལ་འཇོག།

ངེས་ལེགས་ལ་འཁོར་བ་ལས་གྲོལ་བ་ཙམ་གྱི་ཐར་པ་དང་ཐམས་ཅད་མཁྱེན་པ་གཉིས་ལས་དང་པོ་སྒྲུབ་པ་ལས་བརྩམས་ཏེ་གསུངས་པ་ཐམས་ཅད་སྐྱེས་བུ་འབྲིང་དངོས་སམ་དེ་དང་ཐུན་མོང་གི་ཆོས་སྐོར་དུ་འདུ་སྟེ། ལམ་སྒྲོན་དུ། སྲིད་པའི་བདེ་ལས[༣༡] རྒྱབ་ཕྱོགས་ཤིང་། །སྡིག་པའི་ལས་ལས་བཟློག[༣༢] བདག་ཉིད། །གང་ཞིག་རང་ཞི་

ཙམ་དོན་གཉེར། །སྐྱེས་བུ་དེ་ནི་འབྲིང་ཞེས་བྱ། །ཞེས་གསུངས་པ་ལྟར་སྐྱེས་བུ་འབྲིང་ཙམ་ནི་འཁོར་བའི་ཕུན་ཚོགས་ལས་[༡༡] རྒྱབ་ཀྱིས་ཕྱོགས་ནས་འཁོར་བ་སྤངས་པའི་ཐར་པ་ཙམ་རང་དོན་དུ་ཐོབ་བྱར་བྱས་ཏེ་དེའི་ཕྱིར་དུ་བསླབ་པ་གསུམ་ཉམས་སུ་ལེན་པ་ལ་འཇུག་པ་ཞིག་ལ་འདོག།

ཐམས་ཅད་མཁྱེན་པའི་གོ་འཕང་སྒྲུབ་པའི་ཐབས་ལ་ཡང་གསང་སྔགས་དང་ཕར་ཕྱིན་ཐེག་པ་གཉིས་སུ་ཡོད་པ་གཉིས་ཀ་ཡང་སྐྱེས་བུ་ཆེན་པོའི་ཚོས་སྐོར་དུ་འདུས་ཏེ། སྐྱེས་བུ་ཆེན་པོ་དེ་ལམ་སྒྲོན་ལས། རང་རྒྱུད་ཏོག་[༡༩] (གཏོགས་) པའི་སྡུག་བསྔལ་གྱིས། །གང་ཞིག་གཞན་གྱི་སྡུག་བསྔལ་ཀུན། །ཡང་དག་ཟད་པར་ཀུན་ནས་འདོད། །སྐྱེས་བུ་དེ་ནི་མཆོག་ཡིན་ནོ། །ཞེས་གསུངས་པ་ལྟར་སྙིང་རྗེ་ཆེན་པོའི་གཞན་དབང་དུ་གྱུར་པས་སེམས་ཅན་གཞན་གྱིས་སྡུག་བསྔལ་ཀུན་ཟད་པར་བྱ་བའི་ཕྱིར་དུ་སངས་རྒྱས་ཐོབ་བྱར་བྱས་ཏེ་ཕར་ཕྱིན་དྲུག་དང་རིམ་གཉིས་སོགས་ལ་སློབ་པ་ཞིག་ལ་འདོག་པའི་ཕྱིར་རོ།།

གཉིས་པ་སྐྱེས་བུ་གསུམ་གྱི་སྒོ་ནས་འཁྲིད་པའི་རྒྱུ་མཚན་བསྟན་པ་ནི་དེ་ལྟར་སྐྱེས་བུ་གསུམ་དུ་བཤད་ཀྱང་སྐབས་འདིར་སྐྱེས་བུ་ཆེན་པོའི་ལམ་དུ་འཁྲིད་པའི་ཡན་ལག་ཏུ་འོག་མ་གཉིས་ཀྱང་འཁྲེར་ཤེས་དགོས་ལ། དེ་ཡང་སྲིད་པའི་ཕུན་ཚོགས་ཙམ་ལ་ཐོབ་བྱར་བྱེད་པའི་སྐྱེས་བུ་ཆུང་ངུ་ཙམ་དང་། འཁོར་བ་ལས་ཐར་པ་ཙམ་རང་དོན་དུ་ཐོབ་བྱར་བྱེད་པའི་སྐྱེས་བུ་འབྲིང་ཙམ་གྱི་ལམ་དུ་འཁྲིད་པ་མ་ཡིན་གྱི། དེ་གཉིས་དང་ཐུན་མོང་བའི་ལམ་འགའ་ཞིག་སྐྱེས་བུ་ཆེན་པོའི་ལམ་ལ་འཁྲིད་པའི་སྔོན་འགྲོར་བྱས་ནས་དངོས་གཞི་སྐྱེས་བུ་ཆེན་པོའི་ལམ་དུ་འཁྲིད་པ་ཡིན་ལ། དེ་ལྟར་བྱེད་དགོས་པའི་རྒྱུ་མཚན་ནི་ཐེག་ཆེན་དུ་འཇུག་པའི་སྒོ་ནི་བྱང་ཆུབ་མཆོག་ཏུ་སེམས་བསྐྱེད་པ་ལས

གཞན་མེད་པས་བྱང་ཆུབ་ཏུ་སེམས་བསྐྱེད་དགོས་ལ། དེ་ལ་སྔོན་དུ་སེམས་བསྐྱེད་ཀྱི་ཕན་ཡོན་བསམས་ཏེ་སྤྲོ་ཤུགས་འཕེལ་བ་དགོས། སེམས་བསྐྱེད་ཀྱི་ཕན་ཡོན་ཡང་བསྡུ་ན་གནས་སྐབས་ཀྱི་དང་མཐར་ཐུག་གི་ཕན་ཡོན་གཉིས་ལས་གནས་སྐབས་མངོན་མཐོའི་བདེ་འབྲས་ཀྱང་སེམས་བསྐྱེད་ལ་བརྟེན་ནས་བདེ་བླག་ཏུ་འགྲུབ། མཐར་ཐུག་ཐམས་ཅད་མཁྱེན་པའི་གོ་འཕང་ཡང་སེམས་བསྐྱེད་ལ་བརྟེན་ནས་འབྱུང་བས་བྱང་ཆུབ་ཏུ་སེམས་བསྐྱེད་དགོས་ལ། དེ་ལ་ཡང་སེམས་ཅན་ཐམས་ཅད་སྡུག་བསྔལ་གྱིས་མནར་བ་མི་བཟོད་པའི་སྙིང་རྗེ་ཆེན་པོ་སྔོན་དུ་འགྲོ་དགོས། དེ་ལ་རང་སྡུག་བསྔལ་གྱིས་མནར་བ་ལ་མི་འདོད་པའི་བློ་ཤུགས་དྲག་ཅིག་དགོས་པས་ཐོག་མར་ཆུང་ངུའི་སྐབས་ཀྱི་རང་ལ་ངན་སོང་གི་སྡུག་བསྔལ་གྱིས་མནར་ཚུལ་བསམས་ནས་དེ་ལས་ཐར་འདོད་ཀྱི་བློ་དང་། འབྲིང་གི་སྐབས་སུ་མཐོ་རིས་ན་ཡང་བདེ་བ་རང་མཚན་པ་མེད་ཚུལ་བསམས་ནས་འཁོར་བ་མཐའ་དག་ལས་ངེས་པར་འབྱུང་བའི་བློ་བསྐྱེད། དེ་ནས་རང་ཉམས་ལ་དཔགས་ནས་མ་ཀུན་སེམས་ཅན་ཐམས་ཅད་སྡུག་བསྔལ་གྱིས་མནར་བ་ལ་སྒྲོལ་འདོད་ཀྱི་བྱམས་སྙིང་རྗེ་བྱང་ཆུབ་ཀྱི་སེམས་བསྐྱེད་པར་བྱེད་དགོས་པས་ན་ཆུང་འབྲིང་དང་ཐུན་མོང་བའི་བློ་སྦྱོང་བ་ཆེན་པོའི་ལམ་དུ་འཁྲིད་པའི་ཐབས་མཆོག་ཏུ་འགྱུར་བ་ཡིན་པས་སོ།།

གཉིས་པ་སྙིང་པོ་ལེན་ཚུལ་དངོས་ལ་གསུམ་ཡོད་པའི་དང་པོ་ཆུང་ངུ་དང་ཐུན་མོང་བའི་ལམ་ལ་བློ་སྦྱོང་ཚུལ་ནི། བློ་ནང་དུ་ཁྲིལ་ཏེ་བཀུག་ནས། གལ་ཏེ་མི་ལུས་རིན་པོ་ཆེ་རྙེད་དཀའ་ཞིང་རྙེད་ན་དོན་ཆེ་བ་འདི་འདྲ་ཐོབ་འདུག་སྐྱེ་འདི་ཡུན་རིང་དུ་མི་གནས། ངེས་པར་འཆི། དེ་ཡང་ག་ཙམ་[༣༥]ན་འཆི་ངེས་པ་མི་འདུག་པས་ད་ལྟ་ཉིད་ནས་སྙིང་པོ་ལེན་པ་ལ་འབད་དགོས། དེ་ཡང་དེ་སྔ་ཕན་དྲག་ཞན་འབྲིང་གསུམ་འདི་ཙམ་ཞིག་ཁྲིམ་འཁུར་བ་བཞིན་དུ་འཆི་བདག་གིས་བཅོམ། ང་དེ་སྔ་ཕན་མ་ཤི་བ་

དེ་ཡང་ཁར་རྫེ་རེ་ཆེ་ན་སྙམ། སྙིང་ཚ་སྙོང་སྙོང་བ། ས་གཅིག་ཏུ་སྡོད་མི་ཆུགས་པ་ཙམ་གྱི་བློ་ཞིག་བསྐྱེད་ལ། ནོར་ལོངས་སྤྱོད་གཉེན་ཉེ་བ་སུ་གང་དང་ཡང་འགྲོགས་དབང་མེད་པར་དེ་རྣམས་ཀྱི་ཆེད་དུ་བསགས་པའི་སྡིག་པ་དེ་ཁྱེར་ནས་འགྲོ་དགོས་པ་འདི་འདྲ་ནི་ཡ་ཆ་སྙམ་པ་བྱ། ཚེ་འདི་སྣང་གི་བཟའ་དགའ་འཐུང་སྐྱིད། མི་ནོར་ཟས་གསུམ་སོགས་གང་སོང་[༣༦] སོང་སོང་། ད་ངས་ཚེ་ལྷག་གང་ཡོད་འདི་ལ་ཆོས་གཤའ་མ་ཞིག་བྱེད། དེ་ཡང་དེ་རིང་[༣༧] ཉིད་ནས་བྱེད་དགོས་སྙམ་པ་བྱའོ།།

འོ་ན་འཆི་བའི་ཚེ་ཆོས་མ་གཏོགས་གང་གིས་ཀྱང་མི་ཕན་ན། ཤི་བའི་ཚེ་ཆོས་ཀྱིས་ཇི་ལྟར་ཕན། ཆོས་མིན་གྱིས་ཇི་ལྟར་གནོད་སྙམ་ན། ངེད་རང་ཤི་ནས་ཀྱང་མེད་པར་མི་འགྲོ་བར་སྐྱེ་བ་ཞིག་ནི་ླང་དགོས་ཏེ་སྐྱེ་བ་ཡང་བདེ་འགྲོ་དང་ངན་འགྲོ་གང་རུང་ལས་མ་འདས། དེ་ཡང་ལས་ཀྱི་དབང་མ་གཏོགས་རང་དབང་ནི་མེད། ལས་དཀར་ནག་གིས་ཇི་ལྟར་འཕངས་པ་བཞིན་སྐྱེ་དགོས་ལ། དེ་ཡང་འཆི་བའི་ཚེ་དགེ་སེམས་མངོན་དུ་གྱུར་ན་ཕྱི་མ་བདེ་འགྲོར་སྐྱེ། དེའི་ཚེ་མི་དགེ་བའི་སེམས་མངོན་དུ་གྱུར་ན་ཕྱི་མ་ངན་འགྲོ་གསུམ་གང་རུང་དུ་སྐྱེས་ནས་སྡུག་བསྔལ་དྲག་པོ་མྱོང་དགོས།།

ངན་འགྲོ་ན་སྡུག་བསྔལ་ཇི་ལྟར་ཡོད་ན། མགོན་པོ་ཀླུ་སྒྲུབ་ཀྱིས། རབ་ཏུ་ཚ་ཞིང་གྲང་བ་ཡི། །དམྱལ་བ་ཉི་མ་གཅིག་བཞིན་དྲན། །བཀྲེས་སྐོམ་དག་གིས་རིད་པ་ཡི། །ཡི་དྭགས་དག་ཀྱང་དྲན་པར་བྱ། །རྨོངས་པའི་སྡུག་བསྔལ་རབ་མང་བའི། །བྱོལ་སོང་བལྟ་ཞིང་དྲན་པར་བྱ། །དེ་རྒྱུ་རྣམ་སྤང་བདེ་རྒྱུ་སྤྱོད། །འཛམ་བུ་གླིང་གི་མི་ཡི་ལུས། །དེ་ཐོབ་དུས་སུ་ངན་སོང་རྒྱུ། །རབ་ཏུ་བསྒྲིམས་ཏེ་གཅད་[༣༨] པར་བྱ། །ཞེས་གསུངས་པ་ལྟར་དམྱལ་བ་རྣམས་ལ་ཚ་གྲང་གི་སྡུག་བསྔལ་བཟོད་པར་མི་ནུས་པ་ཡོད། ཡི་དྭགས་རྣམས་ལ་བཀྲེས་སྐོམ་གྱི་སྡུག་བསྔལ་བསྲན་མི་ནུས་པ། དུད་འགྲོ་

རྣམས་ལ་གཅིག་ལ་གཅིག་ཟ་སྒྲེན་ལྐུགས་སོགས་ཀྱི་སྡུག་བསྔལ་བཟོད་པར་མི་ནུས་པ་ཡོད། ད་ལྟ་མི་མ་མྱུར་དུ་ལག་པ་བཙུག་ནས་ཡུད་ཙམ་སྡོད་པ་དང་། དགུན་གྲང་སྣང་ལ་གོས་མེད་པར་ཞག་གཅིག་ཙམ་སྡོད་པ་དང་། ཞག་ཁ་ཡར་ཟས་གང་ཡང་མེད་པར་སྡོད་པ་དང་། ལུས་ལ་སྦྲང་བུ་སོགས་ཀྱིས་སོ་བཏབ་པ་ཙམ་ཡང་བཟོད་པར་དཀའ་ན་ཚ་གྲང་གི་དམྱལ་བ་ཡི་དྭགས་དུད་འགྲོ་གཅིག་གིས་གཅིག་གསོན་པོར་མིད་པའི་སྡུག་བསྔལ་སོགས་བདག་གིས་ཇི་ལྟར་བཟོད་སྙམ་དུ་ད་ལྟའི་ཉམས་ལ་དཔགས་ནས་ཤིན་ཏུ་འཇིགས་ཤིང་སྐྲག་པའི་ཡིད་ཀྱི་འགྱུར་བ་མ་ཐོན་བར་དུ་བསྒོམ་ཞིང་། དེས་ན་བདག་གིས་དལ་བའི་རྟེན་བཟང་པོ་ཐོབ་པའི་དུས་འདི་ར་ངན་སོང་གི་རྒྱུ་སྤོང་བ་དང་བདེ་འགྲོའི་རྒྱུ་ལ་འབད་པའི་བློ་ནས་ངན་སོང་དུ་མི་སྐྱེ་བའི་ཐབས་ལ་འབད་པར་བྱའོ་སྙམ་དུ་བསྒོམ།།

འོ་ན་ངན་སོང་དུ་མི་སྐྱེ་བའི་ཐབས་ལ་ཇི་ལྟར་འབད་སྙམ་ན། གོང་དུ་བཤད་པ་ལྟར་ངན་སོང་གི་སྡུག་བསྔལ་གྱིས་འཇིགས་པ་དང་། འཇིགས་པ་དེ་ལས་སྐྱོབ་པའི་ནུས་པ་དཀོན་མཆོག་གསུམ་ལ་ཡོད་པར་ཤེས་ནས་དཀོན་མཆོག་རིན་པོ་ཆེ་རྣམ་པ་གསུམ་ལ་སྙིང་ཐག་པ་ནས་སྐྱབས་སུ་འགྲོ་བར་བྱ་ལ། དཀོན་མཆོག་གསུམ་གྱིས་ངན་སོང་གི་འཇིགས་པ་ལས་སྐྱོབ་ནུས་པ་ཡང་ཡིན་ཏེ། སངས་རྒྱས་དཀོན་མཆོག་དེ་རང་འཇིགས་པ་ཐམས་ཅད་ལས་གྲོལ། གཞན་འཇིགས་པ་ཐམས་ཅད་ལས་སྐྱོབ་པའི་ཐབས་ལ་མཁས། ཀུན་ལ་ཐུགས་རྗེ་ཆེན་པོ་ཉེ་རིང་མེད་པར་འཇུག། ཕན་བཏགས་མ་བཏགས་ཐམས་ཅད་ཀྱི་དོན་མཛད་པས་སྐྱབས་སུ་འོས་ཤིང་། དེས་ཆོས་དང་དགེ་འདུན་ཡང་མཚོན་ནུས་ལ། དེས་ན་ཕྱི་རོལ་པའི་སྟོན་པ་དང་ཆོས་དང་དགེ་འདུན་ལ་ཡོན་ཏན་དེ་དག་གང་ཡང་མེད་པས་སྐྱབས་སུ་མི་འོས། དཀོན་མཆོག་གསུམ་ལ་ཡོན་ཏན་དེ་ལྟར་ཡོད་པས་སྐྱབས་སུ་འགྲོ་བར་འོས་སོ།།

སྐྱབས་སུ་ཇི་ལྟར་འགྲོ་ན། རྐང་གཉིས་རྣམས་ཀྱི་མཆོག་སངས་རྒྱས་ལ་སྐྱབས་སུ་མཆིའོ། བདག་འཁོར་བ་དང་ངན་སོང་གི་སྡུག་བསྔལ་ལས་སྒྲོལ་བའི་སྟོན་པ་མཛད་དུ་གསོལ། འདོད་ཆགས་དང་བྲལ་བ་རྣམས་ཀྱི་མཆོག་ཆོས་ལ་སྐྱབས་སུ་མཆིའོ། བདག་འཁོར་བ་དང་ངན་སོང་གི་འཇིགས་པ་ལས་སྒྲོལ་བའི་སྐྱབས་དངོས་མཛད་དུ་གསོལ། ཚོགས་རྣམས་ཀྱི་མཆོག་དགེ་འདུན་ལ་སྐྱབས་སུ་མཆིའོ། བདག་འཁོར་བ་དང་ངན་སོང་གི་སྡུག་བསྔལ་ལས་སྒྲོལ་བའི་གྲོགས་མཛད་དུ་གསོལ། ཞེས་སྙིང་ཐག་པ་ནས་བློ་ཡིངས་ཏེ་བཀལ་བའི་སྐྱབས་འགྲོ་བྱ།།

དེ་ལྟར་སྐྱབས་སུ་སོང་ནས་བསླབ་བྱ་ལ་མ་བསླབས་ན་སྐྱབས་འགྲོ་ལས་ཉམས་པར་འགྱུར་བས་བསླབ་བྱ་ལ་སློབ་དགོས། དེ་ཡང་བདག་སངས་རྒྱས་ལ་སྐྱབས་སུ་སོང་ནས་འཇིག་རྟེན་པའི་ལྷ་དྲག་པོ་ཁྱབ་འཇུག་སོགས་ལ་སྐྱབས་སུ་མི་འཛིན་སངས་རྒྱས་ཀྱི་སྐུ་གཟུགས་ལ་ཡང་སངས་རྒྱས་དངོས་ཀྱི་འདུ་ཤེས་བྱས་ཏེ་གུས་པར་བྱ། བདག་ཆོས་ལ་སྐྱབས་སུ་སོང་ནས་སེམས་ཅན་ལ་འཚེ་བ་མི་བྱ། ཡི་གེ་ན་གཅིག་ཡན་ཆད་ལ་མ་གུས་པ་སྤངས་ཏེ་གུས་པར་བྱ། བདག་དགེ་འདུན་དཀོན་མཆོག་ལ་སྐྱབས་སུ་སོང་ནས་མུ་སྟེགས་སམ་སྡིག་གྲོགས་དང་འགྲོགས་འདྲིས་མི་བྱ། ཐ་ན་སེར་མོ་[༡༨] གྱོན་ཙམ་ལ་ཡང་མ་གུས་པ་སྤངས་ཏེ་གུས་པར་བྱའོ།།

གཞན་ཡང་ཕན་བདེ་དགེ་ལེགས་ཐམས་ཅད་དཀོན་མཆོག་གི་བཀའ་དྲིན་དུ་ཤེས་པར་བྱས་ཏེ་བཟའ་བཏུང་གི་ཕུད་སོགས་ཀྱིས་དཀོན་མཆོག་ལ་མཆོད་པ་དང་། འཕྲལ་དང་ཕུགས་ཀྱི་དོན་ཐམས་ཅད་དཀོན་མཆོག་གསུམ་ལ་གསོལ་བ་བཏབ་ནས་བྱེད་ཀྱི་ཕལ་པའི་མོ་བོན་སོགས་ལ་མི་བརྟེན། རང་གི་ནུས་པ་གང་ཡོད་ཀྱིས་སེམས་ཅན་གཞན་དཀོན་མཆོག་ལ་སྐྱབས་སུ་འགྲོ་བ་ལ་དགོད། སྲོག་གི་ཕྱིར་ཡང་དཀོན་མཆོག་མི་གཏང་ཞིང་།

དེ་གཏོང་བའི་ཚིག་ཙམ་ཡང་མ་ཤོར་བ་བྱེད་དགོས་ཨང་སྐམ་པ་བྱས་ནས་ཉིན་ལན་གསུམ་མཚན་ལན་གསུམ་དུ་བསམས་ལ། ཡོན་ཏན་ཤེས་པ། ཁྱད་པར་ཤེས་པ། ཁས་བླངས་པ། གཞན་དུ་མི་སྨྲ་བའི་སྒོ་ནས་ཉིན་ལན་གསུམ་མཚན་ལན་གསུམ་དུ་བསམ་པ་ཐག་པ་ནས་སྐྱབས་འགྲོ་བྱའོ།།

འོ་ན་དཀོན་མཆོག་གསུམ་ལ་སྐྱབས་སུ་སོང་བས་[10] ངན་སོང་གི་སྡུག་བསྔལ་ལས་སྐྱོབས་ནུས་མོད། མཐོ་རིས་ཀྱི་རྟེན་འཐོབ་པ་ལ་རྒྱུ་ཇི་ལྟ་བུ་སྒྲུབ་སྐམ་ན། དེ་ཡང་དཀར་ནག་གི་ལས་འབྲས་བསམས་ཏེ་དགེ་སྡིག་གི་ལས་སོ་སོར་ངེས་པ་དང་འཕེལ་ཆེ་བ། ལས་མ་བྱས་པ་དང་མི་འཕྲད་པ། ལས་བྱས་པ་ཆུད་མི་ཟ་བ་སོགས་ཀྱི་ཚུལ་བསམས་ཏེ་དགེ་སྡིག་གི་བླང་དོར་ཚུལ་བཞིན་དུ་བྱེད་དགོས་ལ། དེ་ཡང་དངོས་སྟོབས་ཀྱི་རིགས་པས་ངེས་མི་ནུས་པས་ཏིང་ངེ་འཛིན་རྒྱལ་པོ་ལས[11]། ཟླ་བ་སྐར་མར་བཅས་པ་གནས་ལྷུང་ཞིང་། །རི་དང་གྲོང་དུ་བཅས་པའི་ས་ཞིག་ལ། །ནམ་མཁའི་ཁམས་ནི་རྣམ་པ་གཞན་གྱུར་ཀྱང་། །ཁྱོད་ནི་མི་བདེན་པ་ཡི་ཚིག་མི་གསུང་། །ཞེས་གསུངས་པ་ལྟར་སངས་རྒྱས་ཀྱི་གསུང་ལ་ཞེ་ཐག་པ་ནས་ཡིད་ཆེས་རྙེད་པར་བྱས་ནས། མི་དགེ་བ་ལས་སྡུག་བསྔལ་འབྱུང་། །དེ་ལས་ཇི་ལྟར་ངེས་ཐར་ཞེས། །ཉིན་མཚན་ཀུན་ཏུ་བདག་གིས་ནི། །འདི་ཉིད་འབའ་ཞིག་བསམ་པའི་རིགས[12]། །ཞེས་དང་། དགེ་བའི་ཕྱོགས་རྣམས་ཐམས་ཅད་ཀྱི། །རྩ་བ་མོས་པར་ཐུབ་པས་གསུངས། །དེའི་ཡང་རྩ་བ་རྟག་ཏུ་ནི། །རྣམ་སྨིན་འབྲས་བུ་སྒོམ་པའོ[13]། །ཞེས་གསུངས་པ་ལྟར། སྤྱིར་མི་དགེ་བ་མཐའ་དག་སྤང་། ཁྱད་པར་སྒོ་གསུམ་གྱི་མི་དགེ་བ་བཅུ་ཆེ་འབྲིང་ཆུང་དུར་སྤྱོད་པའི་རྣམ་སྨིན་ངན་སོང་དུ་སྐྱེ་བ། རྒྱུ་མཐུན་དང་བདག་འབྲས་སོགས་ཡིད་དུ་མི་འོང་བ་འབྱིན་ཚུལ་བསམས་ལ། བདེན་པ་པོའི་ལེའུ་ལས[14]། རྒྱལ་པོ་ཁྱོད་ནི་སྲོག་གཅོད་མ་མཛད་

ཅིག །སྐྱེ་བོ་ཀུན་ལ་སྲོག་ནི་རབ་ཏུ་ཕངས། །དེ་བས་ཡུན་རིང་ཚེ་བསྲིང་སུ་འདོད་པ། །ཡིད་ཀྱི་དཀྱུ་ལའང་སྲོག་གཅོད་མི་བསམ་མོ། །ཞེས་གསུངས་པ་ལྟར་སྲོག་གཅོད་པ་སོགས་ཀྱི་ཁ་ན་མ་ཐོ་བ་རྣམས་ལ་ཀུན་སློང་ཙམ་ཡང་མི་རྒྱུ་བར་སྡོམ་སེམས་མང་དུ་བསྐྱེན། སྲོག་གཅོད་སྤོང་བ་སོགས་དགེ་བ་མཐའ་དག་འབད་ནས་སྒྲུབ་དགོས་ཤང་། ཇོ་བླ་མས་ཀྱང་། ཤི་ནས་ངན་འགྲོར་མི་སྐྱེའི་གདེང་[༣༥]མེད་ཅིང་། །དེ་ཡི་འཇིགས་སྐྱོབས་དཀོན་མཆོག་གསུམ་དུ་ངེས། །དེ་ཕྱིར་སྐྱབས་འགྲོ་ཤིན་ཏུ་བསྟེན་[༣༦]པ་དང་། །དེ་ཡི་བསླབ་བྱ་ཉམས་པ་མེད་པར་བྱ། །དེ་ཡང་དཀར་ནག་ལས་འབྲས་ལེགས་བསམས་ཏེ། །བླང་དོར་ཚུལ་བཞིན་སྒྲུབ་ལ་རག་ལས་སོ། །ཞེས་གསུངས།།

དེ་ཡང་མི་དགེ་བཅུ་སྤོང་གི་ཚུལ་ཁྲིམས་བསྲུངས་པས་རྟེན་བཟང་པོ་རྙེད་མོད་ཀྱང་ལམ་མཆོག་རྣམ་མཁྱེན་སྒྲུབ་པ་ལ་རིགས་མཐོ་ཞིང་གཟུགས་བཟང་བ་སོགས་ཀྱི་རྣམ་སྨིན་གྱི་ཡོན་ཏན་བརྒྱད་དང་ལྡན་པ་ཞིག་སྒྲུབ་དགོས་པས་དེའི་རྒྱུ་སེམས་ཅན་ལ་[༣༧]འཚེ་བ་སྤང་བ། མར་མེ་དང་གོས་གསར་པ་སོགས་སྦྱིན་པ། ང་རྒྱལ་བཅོམ་ནས་གཞན་ལ་གུས་པར་བྱ་བ་སོགས་ལ་དྲན་ཤེས་བསྟན་[༣༨](བསྟེན་)ནས་ལག་ཏུ་ལེན་དགོས། འོན་ཀྱང་ཉོན་མོངས་མང་བ་སོགས་ཀྱིས་གལ་ཏེ་སྡིག་ལྟུང་གིས་གོས་ན། དེ་ཊི་མི་སྐམ་པར་མི་འཇོག་པར་ལྟུང་བ་རྣམས་སྐབས་དང་བསྟུན་པའི་ཕྱིར་བཅོས་དང་སྡིག་པ་རྣམས་སྟོབས་བཞི་ཚང་བའི་སྒོ་ནས་བཤགས་པར་བྱས་ལ་སྒོ་གསུམ་སྡིག་ལྟུང་གིས་མ་གོས་པ་ལ་འབད་པར་བྱ་དགོས་ཏེ། ཇོ་བླ་མས་ཀྱང་། ལམ་མཆོག་སྒྲུབ་ལ་མཚན་ཉིད་ཚང་བའི་རྟེན། །མ་རྟེན་བར་དུ་ས་ཆོད་[༣༩]མི་འོང་བས། །དེ་ཡི་མ་ཚང་མེད་པའི་རྒྱུ་ལ་བསླབ། །སྒོ་གསུམ་སྡིག་ལྟུང་དྲི་མས་སྦགས་པ་འདི། །ལྷག་པར་ལས་སྒྲིབ་སྦྱོང་བ་གནད་ཆེ་བས། །རྒྱུན་དུ་སྟོབས་བཞི་ཚང་བ་[༤༠]བསྟེན་པ་གཅེས། །ཞེས་གསུངས་པས་སོ།།

དེ་ལྟར་བསྒོམས་པས་ཚེ་འདི་ལ་བློ་ལོག་སྟེ་ཚེ་ཕྱི་མའི་ཕུན་ཚོགས་དོན་གཉེར་གྱི་བློ་བཅོས་མིན་ནམ་སྐྱེས་པ་ན་སྐྱེས་བུ་ཆུང་ངུའི་ལམ་ལ་བློ་སྦྱངས་པའི་ལག་རྗེས་བྱུང་བ་ཡིན་ནོ།།

གཉིས་པ་སྐྱེས་བུ་འབྲིང་དང་ཐུན་མོང་བའི་ལམ་ལ་བློ་སྦྱོང་བ་ནི། དེ་ལྟར་མི་དགེ་བཅུ་སྤངས་ཤིང་དགེ་བ་བཅུ་ཉམས་སུ་བླངས་པས་མཐོ་རིས་ཀྱི་རྟེན་ཁྱད་པར་ཅན་ཞིག་འཐོབ་མོད་ཀྱང་འཁོར་བའི་སྡུག་བསྔལ་ལས་མ་འདས་པས། དེས་ན་སྡུག་བསྔལ་མཐའ་དག་སྤངས་པའི་ཐར་པ་ཞིག་འཐོབ་དགོས་སོ།།

འོ་ན་འཁོར་བ་མཐའ་དག་སྡུག་བསྔལ་གྱི་རང་བཞིན་ཇི་ལྟར་ཡིན་སྙམ་ན། ངན་སོང་གསུམ་ནི་སྔར་བཤད་པ་ལྟར་ཡིན་ལ། དེ་ཡང་སྐབས་འདིར་ཅུང་ཟད་ཁྱད་པར་བརྗོད་ནས་བསམ་དགོས་པ་ནི་ངན་སོང་སོ་སོའི་སྡུག་བསྔལ་བསམས་ནས་དེའི་རྗེས་ལ། འདི་ལྟ་བུའི་སྡུག་བསྔལ་དར་དྲག་ལ་རྒྱུན་རིང་བ་འདི་བདག་གིས་བཟོད་ཐབས་མི་འདུགས་པས་འདིས་མཚོན་པའི་འཁོར་བའི་སྡུག་བསྔལ་སྤངས་པའི་ཐར་པ་ཅི་ནས་ཀྱང་ཐོབ་པར་བྱ་སྙམ་དུ་བསམ། ངན་སོང་ལས་གཞན་པའི་འཁོར་བ་མཐོ་དམན་མཐའ་དག་ཀྱང་སྡུག་བསྔལ་གྱི་རང་བཞིན་ལས་མ་འདས་ཏེ། མི་རྣམས་ལ་ནི་སྐྱེ་བ་ན་མའི་མངལ་མུན་ནག་དྲི་ང་བ་ལྡུན་ལྡིན་མང་བ་སོགས་ཀྱིས་སྡུག་བསྔལ་ཞིང་། སྐྱེ་བ་ན་ཞག་བདུན་ཕྲག་སོ་བརྒྱད་པ་ལ་སྨིན་ལས་ཀྱི་རླུང་གིས་བདས་ཏེ་འཇུར་མིག་ལ་འདྲེན་པའམ། ཏིལ་བཙིར་བ་ལྟར་ཤིན་ཏུ་སྡུག་བསྔལ་བ་དང་། བཙས་ནས་ཀྱང་ཤིན་ཏུ་འཇམ་པའི་གདན་ལ་བཞག་ཀྱང་ཚེར་མའི་ཁྲོད་དུ་ལྷུང་བ་ལྟ་བུའི་སྡུག་བསྔལ་བཟོད་ཐབས་མེད་པ་ཉམས་སུ་མྱོང་བས་ན་སྐྱེ་བའི་སྡུག་བསྔལ་དེ་ལྟ་བུ་ཡོད།།

བཅས་ནས་ལུས་ལང་ཚོ་དར་ལ་བབ་པར་གྱུར་བ་ནི་རིམ་པས་རྐེད་པ་ནི་གཞུ་ལྟར་གུག །མགོ་བོ་ནི་སྤྲ་བའི་མེ་ཏོག་ལྟར་དཀར། དཔྲལ་བ་ནི་དྲས་སྣན་ལྟར་གཉེར་མས་ཁེངས། སྡོད་པའི་ཚེ་སྒྲེ་ཐག་པ་ཆད་པ་ལྟ་བུ། ལྡང་པའི་ཚེ་ཤིང་རྩ་གནམ་དུ་འདོན་པ་འདྲ་བ། སྨྲ་ན་ལྡེ་ལྡིབ། འགྲོ་ན་[༦༧]ལུས་འབུབ། མིག་རྣ་སོགས་ཀྱིས་ཡུལ་གསལ་བར་མི་མཐོང་། ལུས་ཀྱི་མདངས་ཉམས་པ་ནི་རོ་ལྟ་བུ། དྲན་པ་ཉམས་པས་བརྗེད་ངས་ཆེ། བཟའ་བཏུང་སོགས་འཇུ་དཀའ་ཞིང་ཇི་ལྟར་འདོད་པ་བཞིན་ལོངས་སྤྱོད་མི་ནུས། ཚེ་ཕལ་ཆེར་ཟད་པས་འཆི་བ་ལ་མྱུར་དུ་ཕྱོགས་པའི་རྒ་བའི་སྡུག་བསྔལ་དང་།།

ལུས་ཀྱི་འབྱུང་བ་ཆ་མ་སྙོམས་པར་འཁྲུགས་ཏེ་ན་བའི་ཚེ་ཕྱིའི་པགས་པ་བསྐམས། ནང་གི་ཤ་ཞུ། བཟའ་བཏུང་ཡིད་དུ་འོང་བ་རྣམས་ནད་ལ་ཕོག་དོགས་སྤང་དགོས། ཡིད་དུ་མི་འོང་བའི་བཟའ་བཏུང་སྨན་ལ་སོགས་པ་མི་འདོད་བཞིན་བསྟེན་དགོས། གཏར་སྲེག་སོགས་ཀྱི་དཔྱད་རྩུབ་པོ་རྣམས་བསྟེན་དགོས། ནད་མི་འཚོ་བར་དོགས་ནས་སྡུག་བསྔལ་དཔག་ཏུ་མེད་པ་མྱོང་དགོས་པ་ན་བའི་སྡུག་བསྔལ།།

འཆི་ངེས་པའི་ནད་དྲག་པོས་ཐེབས་ན་འཆི་བར་ཤེས། སྔར་བྱས་ཀྱི་ལས་ངན་རྣམས་ལ་ནི་འགྱོད། མི་ཚེ་སྟོང་ཟད་དུ་སོང་བ་ནི་དྲན། ལུས་ལོངས་སྤྱོད་གཉེན་བཤེས་འཁོར་གཡོག་རྣམས་དང་འབྲལ་བ་ནི་ཤེས། ཁ་ནི་བསྐམས། མཆུ་ནི་བརྗེས། སྣ་ནི་ཞོམ། མིག་ནི་གོང་མོར་སོང་། དབུགས་ནི་རྩེག། ངན་སོང་གི་སྡུག་བསྔལ་དྲག་པོས་ནི་འཇིགས། མི་འདོད་བཞིན་དུ་འཆི་དགོས་པའི་སྡུག་བསྔལ།།

རེས་འགའ་ཚོམ་རྐུན་སོགས་དགྲ་མི་སྡུག་པ་དང་ཕྲད་ནས་ཟས་ནོར་ཐམས་ཅད་བཅོམ། ལུས་ལ་མཚོན་དང་དབྱུག་པ་སོགས་ཀྱིས་བསྣུན། རེས་རྒྱལ་པོ་སོགས་ཀྱི་ཆད་ལས་[༦༨]མི་འདྲ་བ་སྣ་ཚོགས་ཀྱིས་མནར་བ་དང་། ཡང་ན་གཏམ་ངན་ཐོས་པ་

སོགས་ཀྱི་མི་སྡུག་པ་དང་ཕྲད་པའི་སྡུག་བསྔལ། ཟས་ནོར་སོགས་བདེ་སྡུག་གཏམ་ངན་ཁྲིད་དུ་བསད་ནས་བསྒྲུབས་པ་རྣམས་དང་། སྙིང་ཉེ་བ་སོགས་ཡིད་དུ་འོང་བ་དང་མ་འདོད་བཞིན་དུ་འབྲལ་བའི་སྡུག་བསྔལ།

འདོད་པ་བཙལ་ཡང་མ་རྙེད་པའི་སྡུག་བསྔལ་ནི་ཁྱིམ་པ་ལྷ་བུ་ལ་ཞིང་ལས་ལ་འབད་ཀྱང་ཐན་པ་སད་སེར་སོགས་ཀྱིས་ལོ་ཏོག་འདོད་པ་བཞིན་མ་གྲུབ་པ། གྲུ་གཙོང་པའི་ཚོ་རླུང་ལ་སོགས་པས་མ་རུངས་པར་གྱུར་པ། ཚོང་པ་ཡིན་ན་ཚོང་ཟོག་[༩༣]བརླག་པ་ཁེ་ཕྱོགས་མ་བྱུང་བ་སོགས་དང་། རབ་བྱུང་རྣམས་ལ་ནི་ཁས་བླངས་པའི་ཚུལ་ཁྲིམས་མགོ་མ་ཐོན་པ་སོགས་གང་རེ་བ་དེ་མ་ཐོབ་པའི་སྡུག་བསྔལ།།

ཉེར་ལེན་གྱི་ཕུང་པོ་འདི་བླངས་ཙམ་གྱིས་ཚེ་འདིར་ན་ཤ་འཆི་བ་སོགས་སྡུག་བསྔལ་གྱི་རྟེན་བྱེད། ཚེ་ཕྱི་མའི་སྡུག་བསྔལ་རྣམས་འདྲེན་པར་བྱེད། སྡུག་བསྔལ་དང་འགྱུར་བའི་སྡུག་གཉིས་ཀྱི་སྣོད་དུ་གྱུར་པ་དང་། ངོ་བོ་ཁྱབ་པ་འདུ་བྱེད་ཀྱི་སྡུག་བསྔལ་གྱི་རང་བཞིན་ཡིན་པས་སྡུག་བསྔལ་བའི་རང་བཞིན་མ་གཏོགས་བདེ་བའི་རང་བཞིན་ཙུང་ཟད་ཀྱང་མི་འདུག་གོ།།

ལྷ་མིན་ནི་ལུས་བཅད་དྲལ་སོགས་ཀྱི་སྡུག་བསྔལ་ཤིན་ཏུ་རྩུབ་པ་ལས་མ་འདས། འདོད་ལྷ་རྣམས་ལ་ནི་འཆི་ལྟས་ལྔས་ཟིན་པ་ན་དམྱལ་བའི་སྡུག་བསྔལ་ལས་ཆེས་ཆེ་བའི་སྡུག་བསྔལ་དང་། ཕྱ་བཀོང་བ་དང་། གནས་ནས་སྤྲོད་པ་སོགས་སྡུག་བསྔལ་དཔག་ཏུ་མེད་པ་ཡོད། ཁམས་གོང་མའི་ལྷ་སོ་སྐྱེ་ལ་སྡུག་བསྔལ་གྱི་སྡུག་བསྔལ་མངོན་གྱུར་མེད་ཀྱང་། བསམ་གཏན་གསུམ་པ་མན་ཆད་ལ་འགྱུར་བའི་སྡུག་བསྔལ་དང་། བསམ་གཏན་བཞི་པ་དང་། གཟུགས་མེད་ཁམས་སུ་ནི་ཁྱབ་པ་འདུ་བྱེད་ཀྱི་སྡུག་བསྔལ་ཡོལ་མེད་ཀུན་ནས་ཚ་བ་ལྷ་བུའི་སྡུག་བསྔལ་ལས་མ་འདས་འདུག་པས་འཁོར་བ་སྤྱི་བྱེ་བྲག་

གི་སྡུག་བསྔལ་འདི་རྣམས་སྤངས་པའི་ཐར་པའི་གོ་འཕང་ཅི་ནས་ཀྱང་ཐོབ་པར་བྱེད་དགོས་སོ།།

དེ་ཡང་རྒྱུ་མེད་རྐྱེན་མེད་དུ་མི་འཐོབ་པས་ཐར་པ་ཐོབ་བྱེད་ཀྱི་ཐབས་བསླབ་པ་གསུམ་ལ་ཚུལ་བཞིན་དུ་བསླབ་པར་བྱ་དགོས། དེ་ཡང་བསླབ་པ་གཞན་གཉིས་ཀྱི་གཞི་རྟེན་མེད་མི་རུང་ལྷག་པ་ཚུལ་ཁྲིམས་ཀྱི་བསླབ་པ་ལ་བསླབ་དགོས། དེ་ཡང་མི་ཤེས་པ་སོགས་ལྟུང་བ་འབྱུང་བའི་རྒྱུ་རྣམས་ལ་དྲན་ཤེས་ཀྱིས་ལེགས་པར་བརྟགས་ནས་དང་པོར་ལྟུང་བ་མི་འབྱུང་བ་ཞིག་བྱེད། གལ་ཏེ་བྱུང་ཡང་ལྟུང་བ་དང་རྒྱུན་རིང་དུ་མི་འགྲོགས་པར་བཤགས་སྡོམ་ཚུལ་བཞིན་དུ་བྱེད་དགོས། དེས་ན་ཉོན་མོངས་པ་གང་ཆེ་བ་དེའི་གཉེན་པོ་འབད་ནས་བསྒོམས་ཏེ་ལྟུང་བས་མ་གོས་པར་བྱེད་ཅིང་ལས་དང་བྱ་བ་ཅི་བྱེད་ཀྱང་སྟོན་པའི་བཀའ་དང་མི་འགལ་བར་རང་གིས་རང་ལ་མི་ཁྲེལ་བ་ཞིག་བྱེད་དགོས་ཡང་། རྗེ་བླ་མས་ཀྱང་། སྡུག་བདེན་ཉེས་དམིགས་བསམ་ལ་མ་འབད་ན། །ཐར་པ་དོན་གཉེར་ཇི་བཞིན་མི་སྐྱེ་ཞིང་། །ཀུན་འབྱུང་འཁོར་བའི་འཇུག་རིམ་མ་བསམས་ན། །འཁོར་བའི་རྩ་བ་གཅོད་ཚུལ་མི་ཤེས་པས། །སྲིད་ལ་ངེས་འབྱུང་སྐྱོ་ཤས་བསྟེན“པ་དང་། །འཁོར་བར་གང་གིས་བཅིངས་པ་ཤེས་པ་གཅེས། །ཞེས་གསུངས་གདའ་འོ།།

དེས་ན་འཁོར་བ་མཐའ་དག་ལ་མི་འབར་བའི་ཁྱིམ་དུ་ཚུད་པའི་མི་ཞིག་ཁྱིམ་དེ་ལས་ཐར་འདོད་ཡོད་པ་ལྟ་བུའི་འཁོར་བ་ལས་བློ་ལོག་པའི་བློ་སྐྱེས་པ་ན་སྐྱེས་བུ་འབྲིང་གི་ལམ་ལ་བློ་སྦྱངས་པའི་ལག་རྗེས་བྱུང་བ་ཡིན་ནོ།།

གསུམ་པ་སྐྱེས་བུ་ཆེན་པོའི་ལམ་ལ་བློ་སྦྱང་བ་ནི། དེ་ལྟར་ལམ་བསླབ་པ་གསུམ་ཉམས་སུ་བླངས་པས་ཐར་པའི་གོ་འཕང་ཙམ་འཐོབ་ཀྱང་། དེ་ཙམ་གྱིས་མི་ཚོག་སྟེ།

ཐར་པ་ཙམ་ཐོབ་ཕྱིན་ཆད་འཁོར་བར་འཁྱམ་མི་དགོས་ཀྱང་སྐྱོན་ཕྱོགས་རེ་སྤངས་པ་དང་ཡོན་ཏན་ཕྱོགས་རེ་རྫོགས་པ་ཡིན་པས་རང་དོན་མཐར་ཕྱིན་མ་ཐོབ། དེའི་གནད་ཀྱིས་གཞན་དོན་ཡང་ཉི་ཚེ་བ་ལས་མི་འགྲུབ། དེས་ན་དོན་གཉིས་མཐར་ཕྱིན་གྱི་སངས་རྒྱས་ཀྱི་གོ་འཕང་ཞིག་ཐོབ་པར་བྱ་དགོས་པར་འདུག་གོ།

སངས་རྒྱས་དེ་ཡང་རང་ཉིད་རྐྱང་པའི་ཕྱིར་མིན་གྱི། སེམས་ཅན་ཐམས་ཅད་ཀྱི་ཕྱིར་དོན་དུ་གཉེར་བ་ཞིག་དགོས་ཏེ། རང་སྡུག་བསྔལ་གྱི་རྒྱ་མཚོར་ལྷུང་བ་བཞིན་དུ་སེམས་ཅན་རྣམས་ཀྱང་སྡུག་བསྔལ་གྱིས་མནར་བས་ཉམས་ཐག་པ་ཤ་སྟག་ཡིན་ཞིང་། སེམས་ཅན་རྣམས་རང་གི་ཕ་མར་མ་གྱུར་པ་གཅིག་ཀྱང་མེད། དེ་ཡང་ལན་གྲངས་དཔག་ཏུ་མེད་པ་བྱས་ཤིང་དྲིན་གྱིས་བསྐྱངས་པའི་དྲིན་ཅན་འབའ་ཞིག་ཡིན་པས་དྲིན་ཅན་དེ་རྣམས་སྡུག་བསྔལ་ལས་བསྒྲལ་ཏེ། མི་གནས་པའི་མྱང་འདས་བླ་ན་མེད་པའི་གོ་འཕང་ལ་དགོད་པའི་ཕྱིར་དུ་བྱང་ཆུབ་ཀྱི་མཆོག་ཏུ་སེམས་བསྐྱེད་པར་བྱའོ།།

དེ་ཡང་རྒྱུ་འབྲས་མན་ངག་བདུན་གྱི་སྒོ་ནས་བསྐྱེད་དགོས་ཏེ། རྒྱུ་འབྲས་བདུན་ཡང་སེམས་ཅན་ཐམས་ཅད་མར་ཤེས་པ་ལས་དེ་ཐམས་ཅད་ཀྱི་དྲིན་དྲན་པ་འབྱུང་། དེ་ལས་དྲིན་གཟོ། དེ་ལས་ཡིད་འོང་གི་བྱམས། དེ་ལས་ལྷག་བསམ་འདྲེན་ནུས་པའི་བྱམས་པ་དང་སྙིང་རྗེ། དེ་ལས་ལྷག་བསམ་རྣམ་དག །དེ་ལས་བྱང་ཆུབ་ཀྱི་སེམས། དེ་ལས་རྣམ་མཁྱེན་འབྱུང་བའི་ཕྱུགས་བདུན་ཡོད་ལ། དེ་དག་གི་སྔོན་དུ་ཡང་སེམས་ཅན་ཐམས་ཅད་ལ་སེམས་སྙོམས་པའི་བཏང་སྙོམས་སྒོམ་དགོས་ཏེ། སེམས་ཅན་རྣམས་ལ་ཉེ་རིང་བར་མར་ ༄༅ཕྱོགས་སུ་སུ་ལྷུང་བ་ཡོད་ན་སེམས་ཅན་རྣམས་ལ་མར་ཤེས་ཀྱི་བློ་མཚན་ཉིད་ཚང་བ་མི་སྐྱེ། བྱམས་སྙིང་རྗེ་ཙུང་ཟད་སྐྱེ་བ་ཡང་ཕྱོགས་རིས་ཅན་དུ་སྐྱེ་བས་དེས་ན་ཐོག་མར་བཏང་སྙོམས་སྒོམ་དགོས། དེའི་ཚུལ་ཡང་ཚེ་འདིར་ཕན་གནོད་གང་ཡང་

མ་བྱས་པའི་བར་མའི་སེམས་ཅན་དུ་མ་ལ་དམིགས་ནས། འདི་དག་གི་ངོས་ནས་བདེ་བ་འདོད་སྡུག་བསྔལ་མི་འདོད་པར་ཡང་མཚུངས་ཤིང་། རང་གི་ངོས་ནས་འདི་རྣམས་རང་གི་ཕ་མ་བྱས་པའི་གཉེན་ཤ་སྟག་ཡིན་པས་འགའ་རེ་ཉེ་བར་བཟུང་ཕན་འདོགས། འགའ་རེ་རིང་བར་བཟུང་ནས་གནོད་པ་སྐྱེལ་བའི་ཆ་གཉིས་མི་བྱ་བར་འདི་ཐམས་ཅད་ལ་སེམས་མཉམ་པར་བྱའོ་སྙམ་དུ་བསྒོམ། དེ་ནས་ཆེ་འདིའི་གཉེན་ཉེ་བ་རྣམས་དང་། དེ་ནས་ཆེ་འདིར་གནོད་པ་བྱས་པའི་སེམས་ཅན་རྣམས་ལའང་མཉམ་པར་བྱ[༦༨]། དེ་ནས་སེམས་ཅན་ཐམས་ཅད་ལ་སེམས་སྙོམས་པའི་བཏང་སྙོམས་བསྐྱེད་པར་བྱའོ། །དེ་སྐྱེས་པ་དང་འཁོར་བ་ལ་ཐོག་མའི་མཐའ་མེད་པས་ན་བདག་གི་སྐྱེ་བ་ལའང་ཐོག་མའི་མཐའ་མེད། དེའི་གནད་ཀྱིས་གནས་འདི་ལྟ་བུར་མ་སྐྱེས་ཞེས་བྱ་བའམ། སེམས་ཅན་འདི་འདྲ་ཞིག་གིས་བདག་གི་མ་མ་བྱས་ཞེས་བྱ་བ་གཅིག་ཀྱང་མེད། བྱས་པ་ལ་གྲངས་ཀྱིས་ཀྱང་མི་ཚོད། དེས་ན་སྐྱེ་ཤི་འཕོས་པས་ངོ་མ་ཤེས་པ་མ་གཏོགས་སེམས་ཅན་གྱི་ཁམས་ན་རང་གི་ཕ་མར་མ་གྱུར་པ་གཅིག་ཀྱང་མེད། ཕ་མར་གྱུར་རེས་ཀྱིས་ཆེ་འདིའི་མ་དང་འདྲ་བར་དྲིན་གྱིས་བསྐྱངས་པའི་དྲིན་ཅན་ཤ་སྟག་ཡིན།།

ཆེ་འདིའི་མས་དྲིན་གྱིས་ཇི་ལྟར་བསྐྱངས་ན། བདག་གི་ད་ལྟའི་མ་འདིས་མངལ་དུ་ཡོད་པའི་ཆེ་བདག་ལ་གནོད་ཀྱི་དོགས་གཡོར་བཟློ་བ་སོགས་ཀྱིས་བསྐྱངས། བཙས་ནས་ཉེ་འཇམ་པའི་གོས་སྟན་ལ་བཞག །སོར་མོ་བཅུའི་ཁ་ལ་བླངས། བྱམས་པའི་མིག་གིས་བལྟས། དགའ་བའི་འཛུམ་གྱིས་བསུས། བརྩེ་བས་ནུ་ཞོ་བསྣུན། ཤའི་དྲོད་ལ་བཅར། ཟས་ལྕེ་ས་བསྙོད། སྣབས་ཁས་ཕྱིས། མི་གཙང་བ་ལག་པས་ཕྱིས། མ་རང་ཉིད་སྡིག་ལ་ཐུག་པ་བས་ཀྱང་བདག་ཚུང་ཟད་ན་བ་སྡུག་པར་བྱས། དཀའ་ལས་སྐྱིད་སྡུག་ཐམས་ཅད་ཁྲིད་དུ་བསད་ནས་བསྐྱབས་པའི་ནོར་དངོས་པོ་རང་གིས་བེད་གཅོད་

མ་ཉུས་པ་རྣམས་བདག་ལ་བྱིན། མདོར་ན་མ་རང་གི་འཁོས་དང་བསྟུན་པའི་གནོད་འཚེ་ལས་བསྐྱབས། ཕན་བཏགས་པའི་དྲིན་ཅན་ཡིན་སྙམ་པའི་བློ་བརྩེ་ཡམ་ཡམ་པ་བྱ།།

དེ་ནས་ཚེ་འདིའི་ཕ་མ་ལ་སོགས་པའི་གཉེན་ཉེ་བ་རྣམས་དང་། དེ་ནས་བར་མ་རྣམས་དང་། དེ་ནས་ཚེ་འདིར་གནོད་པ་བསྐྱལ་བའི་སེམས་ཅན་ལ་དམིགས་ནས། འདི་རྣམས་ཀྱིས་བདག་གི་མ་བྱས་པ་གྲངས་ཀྱིས་མི་ཆོད། དེ་ཡང་མིའི་རྟེན་ལ་མ་བྱས་པ་གྲངས་ཀྱིས་མི་ཆོད། མ་ནམ་བྱས་རེས་ཀྱིས་ཚེ་འདིའི་མ་བཞིན་དུ་གནོད་པ་ལས་བསྐྱབས། ཕན་ཚད་མེད་པ་བཏགས་པའི་དྲིན་ཅན་ཡིན་ནོ།།

དེ་ལྟར་ལན་གྲངས་ཚད་མེད་པར་དྲིན་གྱིས་བསྐྱངས་པའི་མ་རྣམས་ཉོན་མོངས་པའི་གདོན་གྱིས་སེམས་དཀྲུགས་པས་ཞེས་པ་ལ་རང་དབང་མེད་པར་སྨྱོ། གཏི་མུག་གིས་ཞེས་རབ་ཀྱི་མིག་ལོངས་པས་མངོན་མཐོ་ངེས་ལེགས་ཀྱི་ལམ་ལྟ་བའི་མིག་དང་ནི་བྲལ། ཐར་པའི་གྲོང་དུ་འཁྲིད་པའི་དགེ་བའི་བཤེས་གཉེན་གྱི་ཡོང་འཁྲིད་པ་ནི་མེད། སྐད་ཅིག་རེ་རེ་ཞིང་ཉེས་སྤྱོད་ཀྱིས་དབྱེན་བཅོས་ནས་གོམ་འཁྲོས་འཁྱོར་བས་འཁོར་བ་དང་ངན་སོང་གི་གཡང་ས་ཉམ་ང་བར་འགྲིམ་པས་སྡུག་བསྔལ་ཞིང་ཉམ་ཐག་པ་འདི་རྣམས་བུ་བདག་ལ་མི་རེ་ན་སུ་ལ་རེ། མ་དེ་སྡུག་བསྔལ་ལས་སྒྲོལ་བ་ཡང་བདག་ལ་མི་འབབ་ན་སུ་ལ་འབབ། དྲིན་ཅན་གྱི་མ་རྣམས་ཡལ་བར་དོར་ནས་རང་གཅིག་པུ་འཁོར་བ་ལས་ཅི་ཐར་བྱེད་ན་དེ་ལས་ཁྲེལ་དང་ངོ་ཚ་ཆུང་བ་མི་འོང་། དེས་ན་མ་རྣམས་ཀྱིས་འཁོར་བའི་བདེ་འབྲས་ཚངས་པ་དང་བརྒྱ་བྱིན་སོགས་ཇི་སྙེད་ཅིག་ཐོབ་ཀྱང་རྟག་མ་ཐུབ། ད་བདག་གིས་རང་ཡལ་བར་དོར་ནས་ནམ་མཁའ་དང་མཉམ་པའི་སེམས་ཅན་ཐམས་ཅད་འཁོར་བའི་སྡུག་བསྔལ་ལས་བསྒྲལ་ཏེ་ཐར་པ་བླ་ན་མེད་པའི་བདེ་བ་ལ་ཅི་ནས་ཀྱང་དགོད་པར་བྱའོ།།

དེས་ན་བདེ་བས་ཕོངས་པའི་མ་རྒན་འདི་རྣམས་ཐམས་ཅད་བདེ་བ་དང་ལྡན་ན་ཅི་མ་རུང་། བདེ་བ་དང་ལྡན་པར་གྱུར་ཅིག །ཅི་ནས་ཀྱང་བདེ་བ་དང་ལྡན་པར་བྱའོ། །སྡུག་བསྔལ་གྱིས་མནར་བའི་མ་རྒན་སེམས་ཅན་འདི་ཐམས་ཅད་སྡུག་བསྔལ་དང་བྲལ་ན་ཅི་མ་རུང་། སྡུག་བསྔལ་དང་བྲལ་བར་གྱུར་ཅིག །སྡུག་བསྔལ་དང་བྲལ་བར་བྱའོ། །དེ་ཡང་བདག་གིས་བྱའོ།།

འོ་ན་དེའི་ནུས་པ་ཁྱོད་ལ་ཡོད་དམ་སྙམ་ན། ད་ལྟ་ནི་བདག་ལ་སེམས་ཅན་ཐམས་ཅད་ལྟ་ཞོག །སེམས་ཅན་གཅིག་ཙམ་ཡང་འཁོར་བའི་སྡུག་བསྔལ་ལས་བསྒྲལ་ནས་བདེ་བ་བླ་ན་མེད་པ་ལ་འགོད་པའི་ནུས་པ་མི་འདུག །དེ་ལྟར་དམ་བཅའ་ཞིག་ནི་བྱས། ད་དམ་བཅའ་དེ་ཡལ་བར་དོར་ན་ངན་སོང་དུ་ལྟུང་བར་འགྱུར་བས། དེས་ན་སེམས་ཅན་ཐམས་ཅད་སྡུག་བསྔལ་ལས་སྒྲོལ་བ་དང་བདེ་བ་བླ་ན་མེད་པ་ལ་འགོད་ནུས་པ་སངས་རྒྱས་མ་གཏོགས་གཞན་ན་མི་འདུག་པས་བདག་གིས་སེམས་ཅན་ཐམས་ཅད་སྡུག་བསྔལ་མཐའ་དག་ལས་བསྐྱབས་ནས་བླ་ན་མེད་པའི་བདེ་བ་ལ་དགོད་པའི་དོན་དུ་ཡང་དག་པར་རྫོགས་པའི་སངས་རྒྱས་ཀྱི་གོ་འཕང་ཅི་ནས་ཀྱང་ཐོབ་པར་བྱའོ་སྙམ་དུ་བསམ།།

དེ་ལྟར་སྨོན་པ་ཙམ་གྱིས་མི་ཚིག་པས་བསམ་པ་སེམས་བསྐྱེད་དེ། ཚེ་འདིར་མི་ཉམས་པའི་རྒྱུར་སེམས་བསྐྱེད་ལ་སྦྱོ་ཤུགས་འཕེལ་བའི་ཕྱིར་དུ་ཕན་ཡོན་དྲན་པ་ལ་བསླབ་པ། སེམས་བསྐྱེད་དངོས་འཕེལ་བའི་ཕྱིར་དུ་ལན་དྲུག་ཏུ་བསྐྱེད་པ་ལ་བསླབ་པ། གང་གི་དོན་དུ་སེམས་བསྐྱེད་པའི་སེམས་ཅན་བློས་མི་སྤོང་[༤༧](བ་)ལ་བསླབ་པ། ཚོགས་བསག་པ་ལ་བསླབ་པ་དང་བཞི་ལས།།

དང་པོ་ནི་བྱང་ཆུབ་ཏུ་སེམས་བསྐྱེད་པ་ཙམ་གྱིས་ལྷ་མི་ཐམས་ཅད་ཀྱི་མཆོད་པའི་གནས་སུ་འགྱུར། ཉན་རང་དགྲ་བཅོམ་རྣམས་ཀྱང་རིགས་ཀྱི་སྒོ་ནས་ཟིལ་གྱིས

གནོན། རིམས་ལ་སོགས་པའི་ནད་དང་གདོན་གྱིས་མི་ཚུགས་ཤིང་། ཞི་སོགས་ཀྱི་ལས་རྣམས་ཀྱང་ཆོགས་མེད་དུ་འགྲུབ། ངན་སོང་ལ་སོགས་པར་མི་སྐྱེ། སྐྱེས་ཀྱང་མྱུར་དུ་ཐར། སྡིག་པ་སྟོབས་ཅན་ཤིན་ཏུ་ཆེ་བ་ཡང་མྱུར་དུ་འཛོམས། བྱང་ཆུབ་ཀྱི་སེམས་བསྐྱེད་པའི་ཕན་ཡོན་གཟུགས་སུ་གྲུབ་ན་ནི་ནམ་མཁར་མི་ཤོང་བར་བཤད་པས་སེམས་འདི་མི་ཉམས་པར་གོང་འཕེལ་དུ་བྱེད་དགོས་སྙམ་དུ་བསམ།།

གཉིས་པ་ནི། བདག་གིས་བྱང་ཆུབ་ཀྱི་སེམས་འདི་བར་མ་དོར་བཏང་ན་ཕམ་ཡས་ཀྱང་ནམ་སྨིན་ཕྱི་པས་སངས་རྒྱས་མ་ཐོབ་པར་དུ་མི་གཏོང་ཞིང་། ཉིན་ལན་གསུམ་མཚན་ལན་གསུམ་དུ། སངས་རྒྱས་ཆོས་དང་ཚོགས་ཀྱི་མཆོག་རྣམས་ལ། །བྱང་ཆུབ་བར་དུ་བདག་ནི་སྐྱབས་སུ་མཆི། །བདག་གི་སྦྱིན་སོགས་བགྱིས་པ་འདི་དག་གིས། །འགྲོ་ལ་ཕན་ཕྱིར་སངས་རྒྱས་འགྲུབ་པར་ཤོག །ཅེས་པ་ལན་གསུམ་གསུམ་གྱིས་སེམས་བསྐྱེད་པར་བྱའོ།།

གསུམ་པ་ནི་དག་གིས་སེམས་ཅན་གྱི་དོན་དུ་བྱང་ཆུབ་ཀྱི་སེམས་བསྐྱེད་པ་ཡིན་པས་སེམས་ཅན་གྱི་ངོས་ནས་མི་འདྲ་བ་ཅི་བྱུང་ཡང་བདག་རང་གི་ངོས་ནས་སེམས་ཅན་ཐམས་ཅད་ནམ་དུའང་བློས་མི་སྤང་སྙམ་པ་བྱའོ།།

བཞི་པ་ནི། བྱང་ཆུབ་ཀྱི་སེམས་ལན་གཅིག་བསྐྱེད་པ་འདི་མི་ཉམས་ཤིང་གོང་ནས་གོང་དུ་འཕེལ་བའི་ཕྱིར་དུ་དཀོན་མཆོག་མཆོད་པ་སོགས་ཚོགས་རྒྱ་ཆེན་པོ་ལ་བསླབ་པར་བྱའོ།།

སྐྱེ་བ་གཞན་དུ་ཡང་བྱང་ཆུབ་ཀྱི་སེམས་དེ་དང་མི་འབྲལ་བའི་རྒྱུར་ནི་ནག་པོའི་ཆོས་བཞི་སྤོང་བ་དང་དཀར་པོའི་ཆོས་བཞི་བསྟེན་པ་ལ་བསླབ་དགོས་པའི་ནག་པོའི་ཆོས་བཞི་ནི། དང་པོ་མཁན་པོ་དང་བླ་མ་སོགས་ཡོན་གནས་གང་ཡང་རུང་བ་ལ་རྫུན་

གྱིས་དབུ་སྐོར་ཐབས་བྱེད་པ་ནག་ཆོས་ཡིན་པས་དེ་འདྲ་གཏན་མི་བྱ་ཞིང་དེའི་གཉེན་པོར་སེམས་ཅན་སུ་ལ་འང་སྲོག་གམ་གཞན་[66] གད་ཀྱི་ཕྱིར་ཡང་རྫུན་མི་སྨྲ།།

ནག་ཆོས་གཉིས་པ་གཞན་དགེ་བ་བསྒྲུབས་ནས་མི་འགྱོད་པ་ལ་འགྱོད་དུ་གཞུག་པ་སྟེ། དེ་ལྟ་བུ་གཏན་མི་བྱ་ཞིང་། དེའི་གཉེན་པོར་རང་གིས་སྨིན་པར་བྱ་བའི་གདུལ་བྱ་སྣོད་དུ་རུང་ན་ཐེག་དམན་ལ་མི་འགོད་པར་ཐེག་ཆེན་ལ་འགོད་པར་བྱའོ།།

ནག་ཆོས་གསུམ་པ་ཐེག་པ་ཆེན་པོར་སེམས་བསྐྱེད་པའི་གང་ཟག་ལ་ཞེ་སྡང་གིས་མི་སྙན་པ་རྗོད་[67] (བརྗོད་) པ་སྟེ། དེ་འདྲ་གཏན་མི་བྱ་ཞིང་དེའི་གཉེན་པོར་ཐེག་ཆེན་གྱི་གང་ཟག་ལ་སྟོན་པའི་འདུ་ཤེས་བསྐྱེད། སྐབས་སུ་བབ་ན་དོན་ལ་གནས་པའི་བསྔགས་པ་བརྗོད་ཅིང་སེམས་ཅན་ཐམས་ཅད་ལ་ཡང་དག་སྣང་སྦྱང་བར་བྱའོ།།

ནག་ཆོས་བཞི་པ་ནི་སེམས་ཅན་ལ་གཡོ་སྒྱུ་སྤྱོད་པར་བྱེད་པ་སྟེ། དེ་འདྲ་ནམ་ཡང་མི་བྱ་ཞིང་སེམས་ཅན་རྣམས་ལ་དྲང་པོའི་བསམ་པ་བྱའོ། །རྗེ་བླ་མས་ཀྱང་། སེམས་བསྐྱེད་ཐེག་ཆེན་[68] ལམ་གྱི་གཞུང་ཤིང་སྟེ། །རླབས་ཆེན་སྤྱོད་པ་རྣམས་ཀྱི་གཞི་དང་རྟེན། །ཚོགས་གཉིས་ཀུན་ལ་གསེར་འགྱུར་རྩི་ལྟ་བུ། །རབ་འབྱམས་དགེ་ཚོགས་སྡུད་པའི་བསོད་ནམས་གཏེར། །དེ་ལྟར་ཤེས་ནས་རྒྱལ་སྲས་དཔའ་བོ་རྣམས། །རིན་ཆེན་སེམས་མཆོག་ཐུགས་དམ་མཐིལ་དུ་འཛིན། །ཞེས་གསུངས།།

འོ་ན་སྨོན་སེམས་ལ་བསླབས་པ་ཙམ་གྱིས་ཆོག་གམ་སྙམ་ན། དེ་ཙམ་གྱིས་མི་ཆོག། དེའི་སྟེང་དུ་འཇུག་སྡོམ་བླངས་ནས་རྒྱལ་སྲས་ཀྱི་སྤྱོད་པ་རླབས་པོ་ཆེ་ལ་བསླབ་དགོས་ཤིང་། དེ་ཡང་རང་རྒྱུད་སྨིན་བྱེད་ཕར་ཕྱིན་དྲུག་དང་། གཞན་རྒྱུད་སྨིན་བྱེད་བསྡུ་བའི་དངོས་པོ་བཞི་ལ་བསླབ་དགོས་པའི་དང་པོ་ལ་དྲུག་ཡོད་པ་ལས། སྦྱིན་པ་ལ་བསླབ་ཚུལ་ནི། སེམས་ཅན་ཐམས་ཅད་ཀྱི་ཕྱིར་དུ་སངས་རྒྱས་ཐོབ་པར་བྱའོ་སྙམ་པའི་

བསམ་པ་དེས་ཀུན་ནས་བསླང་སྟེ་དམ་པའི་ཆོས་ཀྱིས་ཕོངས་པ་ཐམས་ཅད་ལ་དམ་པའི་ཆོས་ཕྱིན་ཅི་མ་ལོག་པ་བསྟན། རྒྱལ་པོ་དང་དམག་ལ་སོགས་པའི་འཇིག་པ་དང་། འདྲེ་གཅན་གཟན་སྦྲུལ་ལ་སོགས་པའི་སེམས་ཡོད་ཀྱི་འཇིགས་པ། མི་ཆུ་སོགས་སེམས་མེད་ཀྱི་འཇིགས་པ་རྣམས་ལས་བསྐྱབ། བཟའ་བཏུང་མལ་སྟན་ན་བའི་གསོས་སྨན་སོགས་ནོར་གྱིས་ཕོངས་པ་རྣམས་ལ་དེ་དག་ཕངས་མེད་དུ་སྦྱིན། མདོར་ན་ལུས་ལོངས་སྤྱོད་དུས་གསུམ་དུ་བསགས་པའི་དགེ་རྩ་ཐམས་ཅད་ཕངས་མེད་དུ་གཏང་ངོ་། །དེ་ལྟར་ཡང་རྗེ་བླ་མས། སྦྱིན་པ་འགྲོ་བའི་རེ་སྐོང་ཡིད་བཞིན་ནོར། །སེར་སྣའི་མདུད་པ་གཅོད་པའི་མཚོན་ཆ་མཆོག །མ་ཞུམ་སྙིང་སྟོབས་བསྐྱེད་པའི་རྒྱལ་སྲས་སྤྱོད། །སྙན་པའི་གྲགས་པ་ཕྱོགས་བཅུར་སྒྲོག་པའི་གཞི། །དེ་ལྟར་ཤེས་ནས་ལུས་དང་ལོངས་སྤྱོད་དགེ །ཡོངས་སུ་གཏོང་བའི་ལམ་བཟང་མཁས་པས་བསྟེན། །ཞེས་གསུངས།།

གཉིས་པ་ཚུལ་ཁྲིམས་ལ་བསླབ་ཚུལ་ནི། སེམས་ཅན་གྱི་དོན་དུ་སངས་རྒྱས་ཐོབ་པར་བྱ། དེའི་ཕྱིར་དུ་དྲན་ཤེས་བཞིན་ངོ་ཚ་ཁྲེལ་ཡོད་ཀྱི་བསམ་པ་ན་རེ་བྱས་ལ་མི་དགེ་བ་སྤྲོག་ལ་བབ་ཀྱང་མི་བྱ་ཞིང་། དེ་ལྟར་ཉེས་སྤྱོད་སྡོམ་པའི་ཚུལ་ཁྲིམས་དེ་ལ་བརྟེན་ནས་ཕར་ཕྱིན་དྲུག་གོང་འཕེལ་དུ་བྱེད་དགོས། དེ་གཉིས་ལ་བརྟེན་ནས་སེམས་ཅན་གྱི་དོན་ཁ་ན་མ་ཐོ་བ་མེད་པར་བསྒྲུབ་ཏེ་ཚུལ་ཁྲིམས་གསུམ་ལ་བསླར་པར་བྱ་སྟེ། རྗེ་བླ་མས། ཚུལ་ཁྲིམས་ཉེས་སྤྱོད་དྲི་མ་འཁྲུད་པའི་ཆུ། །ཉོན་མོངས་ཚ་གདུང་སེལ་བ་ཟླ་བའི་འོད། །སྐྱེ་རྒུའི་[༥༡]དབུས་ན་ལྷུན་པོ་ལྟ་བུར་བརྗིད། །སྟོབས་ཀྱིས་བསྡིགས་པ་མེད་པར་འགྲོ་ཀུན་འདུད། །དེ་ལྟར་ཤེས་ནས་ཡང་དག་བླངས་པའི་ཁྲིམས། །དམ་པ་རྣམས་ཀྱིས་མིག་བཞིན་སྲུང་[༥༢]བར་མཛད། །ཅེས་གདམས།

བཟོད་པ་ལ་བསླབ་ཚུལ་ལ། གཞན་གྱིས་རང་ལ་གནོད་པ་བྱས་པ་ལ་ཁྲོ་བར་མི་འོས་ཏེ། གཞན་གྱིས་གནོད་པ་བྱས་པ་དེ་སྔར་རང་གིས་ཁོ་ལ་གནོད་པ་བསྐྱལ་བའི་ལེ་ལན་ཡིན་ཞིང་། ཁོ་རང་ཡང་ཁོང་ཁྲོས་རང་དབང་མེད་པར་བྱས་པ་ཡིན་པས་གནོད་ལན་བྱེད་མི་རུང་། ཁོང་ཁྲོ་སྐད་ཅིག་མ་རེས་ཀྱང་བསྐལ་པ་མང་པོར་བསགས་པའི་གཞི་གསུམ་གྱི་དགེ་རྩ་རྣམས་འཛོམས་པར་འདུག་པས་བདག་གིས་ཁོང་ཁྲོའི་བསམ་པ་ཡིད་ཀྱི་དགུ་ལའང་མི་བྱ་ཨང་སྙམ་གནོད་པ་ལ་ཧ་མི་སྙམ་པའི་བཟོད་པ་དང་། གཞན་གྱིས་བདག་ལ་གནོད་པ་བྱས་ནས་སྡུག་བསྔལ་དྲག་པོ་མྱོང་བས་ཉེ་ང་རྒྱལ་དང་དྲེགས་པ་སོགས་སེལ། འཁོར་བ་ལས་ངེས་པར་འབྱུང་བའི་བློ་སྐྱེ། སྡུག་བསྔལ་མི་འདོད་པ་བྱུང་བ་ན། དེ་མི་དགེ་བ་ལས་བྱུང་བ་ཡིན་པས་རྒྱུ་མེད་ན་འབྲས་བུ་ག་ལ་འབྱུང་སྙམ་དུ་མི་དགེ་བ་ལ་མི་འཇུག །གཞན་གྱིས་གནོད་པ་བྱས་པ་ལ་བཟོད་པ་བསྒོམས་པས་ཕྱིན་དྲུག་གཞན་རྣམས་ཀྱང་རྫོགས་ནས་འཚང་རྒྱ་བས་གནོད་བྱེད་ལ་བཟོད་པ་བསྒོམ་པའི་གདམས་ངག་སྙེར་བའི་བླ་མ་ལྟ་བུར་མཐོང་ནས་དྲིན་ཆེ་བའི་བློ་སྐྱེད་པ་སྡུག་བསྔལ་དང་ལེན་གྱི་བཟོད་པ་དང་། དཀོན་མཆོག་གསུམ་དང་སངས་རྒྱས་བྱང་སེམས་ཀྱི་མཐུ་བསམ་གྱིས་མི་ཁྱབ་པ་མཐོང་སྟེ་རྒྱལ་སྲས་ཀྱི་སྤྱོད་པ་དང་བདག་མེད་པའི་དོན་ལ་མོས་པའི་བློ་ནས་དེ་རྣམས་ལ་སློབ་འདོད་ཆོས་ལ་ངེས་སེམས་ཀྱི[༥༣]བཟོད་པའི་ཉམས་ལེན་ཞི་ཐག་པ་ནས་བྱེད་དགོས་ཏེ། རྗེ་བླ་མས། བཟོད་པ་སྟོབས་ལྡན་རྣམས་ལ་རྒྱན་གྱི་མཆོག །ཉོན་མོངས་གདུང་བའི་དཀའ་ཐུབ་ཀུན་གྱི་ཕུལ། །ཞེ་སྡང་ལག་འགྲོའི་དགྲ་ལ་ནམ་མཁའ་ལྡིང་། །ཚིག་རྩུབ་མཚོན་ལ་སྲ་བའི་གོ་ཆ་ཡིན། །དེ་ལྟར་ཤེས་ནས་བཟོད་མཆོག་གོ་ཆ་ལ། །རྣམ་པ་སྣ་ཚོགས་ཚུལ་གྱིས་གོམས་པར་མཛད། །ཅེས་གསུངས་སོ།།

བཞི་པ་བརྩོན་འགྲུས་ལ་བསླབ་ཚུལ་ནི། སྒོ་གསུམ་གྱི་སྡོམ་ལས་དང་འཁྲིག་པ་དང་གཉིད་ཀྱི་བདེ་བ་སོགས་བདེ་བ་དམན་པ་ལ་སྲེད་པ་ལ་འཁོར་བ་ལ་སྐྱོ་བ་མ་བསྒོམས་པ་ལས་ལེ་ལོ་སྐྱེ་བས་ལེ་ལོའི་རྒྱུ་དེ་རྣམས་སྤངས་ཏེ་ལུས་ངག་ཡིད་གསུམ་དགེ་བའི་བྱ་བ་འབའ་ཞིག་གིས་འཁོལ་དགོས། དེ་ཡང་སེམས་ཅན་གཅིག་ཙམ་གྱི་སྡུག་བསྔལ་སེལ་བའི་ཕྱིར་དུ་ཡང་དཀའ་སྤྱད་ལུས་སྲོག་ལ་མི་བལྟ་སྙམ་པ་གོ་ཆའི་བརྩོན་འགྲུས། དེ་ལ་བརྟེན་ནས་ཕར་ཕྱིན་དྲུག་གི་ཉམས་ལེན་གོང་འཕེལ་དུ་བྱེད་པ་དགེ་བ་ཆོས་སྡུད་ཀྱི་བརྩོན་འགྲུས། དེ་གཉིས་ཀྱི་སྒོ་ནས་ཁ་ན་མ་ཐོ་བ་མེད་པའི་སེམས་ཅན་གྱི་དོན་འབད་ནས་བྱེད་པ་སེམས་ཅན་དོན་བྱེད་ཀྱི་བརྩོན་འགྲུས་ལ་འབད་དགོས་ཏེ། རྗེ་བླ་མས། མི་ལྡོག་[༥༤] བརྟན་པའི་བརྩོན་འགྲུས་གོ་བགོས་ན། །ལུང་རྟོགས་ཡོན་ཏན་ཡར་ངོའི་ཟླ་བཞིན་འཕེལ། །སྤྱོད་ལམ་ཐམས་ཅད་དོན་དང་ལྡན་པར་གྱུར།[༥༥] །གང་བརྩམས་ལས་ཀྱི་མཐའ་རྣམས་ཡིད་བཞིན་འགྲུབ། །དེ་ལྟར་ཤེས་ནས་ལེ་ལོ་ཀུན་སེལ་བའི། །རླབས་ཆེན་བརྩོན་འགྲུས་རྒྱལ་སྲས་རྣམས་ཀྱིས་བརྩམ།[༥༦] །ཞེས་གསུངས་སོ།།

ལྔ་པ་བསམ་གཏན་ལ་བསླབ་ཚུལ་ནི། སེམས་བསྐྱེད་ཀྱིས་ཀུན་ནས་བསླང་སྟེ་འཇིག་རྟེན་དང་འཇིག་རྟེན་ལས་འདས་པའི་བསམ་གཏན་གཉིས་དང་། ཕྱོགས་ཀྱི་དབྱེ་བས་ཞི་གནས་དང་ལྷག་མཐོང་ཞི་ལྷག་ཟུང་འབྲེལ་གྱི་བསམ་གཏན་གསུམ་དང་། བྱེད་ལས་ཀྱི་སྒོ་ནས་མཐོང་ཆོས་ཚེ་འདི་ལ་ལུས་སེམས་བདེ་བར་གནས་པའི་བསམ་གཏན། མངོན་ཤེས་སོགས་ཡོན་ཏན་གོང་མ་མངོན་པར་སྒྲུབ་པའི་བསམ་གཏན། སེམས་ཅན་གྱི་དོན་སྒྲུབ་པའི་བསམ་གཏན་དང་གསུམ་སྟེ། དེ་རྣམས་ལ་བྱིང་རྒོད་དང་བྲལ་བར་བསླབ་པར་བྱ་དགོས་ཏེ། རྗེ་བླ་མས། བསམ་གཏན་སེམས་ལ་དབང་སྒྱུར་[༥༧] རྒྱལ་པོ་སྟེ། །བཞག་ན་གཡོ་མེད་རི་ཡི་དབང་པོ་བཞིན། །བཏང་ན་དགེ་བའི་དམིགས་པ་ཀུན་

ལ་འཇུག །ལུས་སེམས་ལས་སུ་རུང་བའི་བདེ་ཆེན་འདྲེན། །དེ་ལྟར་ཤེས་ནས་རྣལ་འབྱོར་དབང་པོ་རྣམས། །རྣམ་གཡེང་དགྲ་འཇོམས་ཏིང་འཛིན་རྒྱུན་དུ་བསྟེན། །ཞེས་གསུངས།།

དྲུག་པ་ཤེས་རབ་ལ་བསླབ་ཚུལ་ནི། སེམས་བསྐྱེད་ཀྱིས་ཀུན་ནས་བསླང་སྟེ། སྲིད་པའི་རྩ་བ་དྲུངས་ནས་འབྱིན་བྱེད་དེ་ཁོ་ན་ཉིད་ཀྱི་དོན་རྟོགས་པ་དོན་དམ་རྟོགས་པའི་ཤེས་རབ་དང་། ཀུན་རྫོབ་རྟོགས་པའི་ཤེས་རབ་དང་། དེ་གཉིས་ཀྱིས་སེམས་ཅན་གྱི་དོན་བྱེད་པའི་ཤེས་རབ་རྣམས་ལ་བསླབ་པར་བྱ་དགོས་ཏེ། རྗེ་བླ་མས། ཤེས་རབ་ཟབ་མོའི་དེ་ཉིད་ལྟ་བའི་མིག །སྲིད་པའི་རྩ་བ་དྲུང[༥༦](དྲུངས་)ནས་འབྱིན་པའི་ལམ། །གསུང་རབ་ཀུན་ལས་བསྔགས་པའི་ཡོན་ཏན་གཏེར། །གཏི་མུག་མུན་སེལ་སྒྲོན་མེ་མཆོག་ཏུ་གྲགས། །དེ་ལྟར་ཤེས་ནས་ཐར་འདོད་མཁས་པ་ཡིས། །ལམ་དེ་འབད་པ་དུ་མས་བསྐྱེད་པར་མཛད། །ཅེས་གསུངས་སོ།།

གཉིས་པ་གཞན་རྒྱུད་སྨིན་བྱེད་བསྡུ་བ་བཞི་ལ་བསླབ་ཚུལ་ནི། སེམས་ཅན་གྱི་དོན་དུ་སངས་རྒྱས་ཐོབ་པར་བྱ་སྙམ་པའི་བསམ་པ་དེས་ཀུན་ནས་བསླང་སྟེ་ཐོག་མར་ཟང་ཟིང་གི་སྦྱིན་པས་སེམས་ཅན་རྣམས་འཁོར་དུ་བསྡུས། དེ་ནས་སེམས་ཅན་རྣམས་དགའ་བའི་ཕྱིར་དུ་བཞིན་མདངས་གསལ་བ་སྔོན་དུ་བཏང་སྟེ་ཕེབས་པར་སྨྲ་བས་བག་ཕབ། དེ་ནས་ཕྱིན་དྲུག[༥༧]གི་གཏམ་ལ་སོགས་པ་ཆོས་སྙན་པར་སྨྲ་བ་དང་། དེ་ནས་ཆོས་བསྟན་པ་ལྟར་དོན་ཉམས་སུ་ལེན་དུ་འཇུག་པའི་དོན་སྤྱོད་པ་དང་། དེ་ནས་གཞན་ལ་ཇི་ལྟར་ཉམས་སུ་ལེན་དུ་བཅུག་པ་ལྟར་རང་ཉིད་ཀྱང་ཕར་ཕྱིན་དྲུག་ཉམས་སུ་ལེན་པའི་དོན་མཐུན་པ་སྟེ། གཞན་དོན་སྒྲུབ་པའི་ཐབས་ཟབ་མོ་འདི་རྣམས་ལ་ཅི་ནས་ཀྱང་བསླབ་པར་བྱ་ལ།།

དེ་ས་ན་བདག་འཛིན་འཁོར་བའི་རྩ་བ་ཡིན་པས་དེ་དང་འཛིན་སྟངས་དངོས་སུ་འགལ་བའི་ལམ་སྒོམ་པ་མེད་པར་རྩེ་གཅིག་པའི་བསམ་གཏན་ཙམ་གྱིས་འཁོར་བའི་རྩ་བ་གཅོད་མི་ནུས་ཤིང་། དམིགས་པ་ལས་མི་གཡོ་བར་རྩེ་གཅིག་ཏུ་གནས་པའི་ཞི་གནས་མེད་པར་བདེན་མེད་རྟོགས་པའི་ཤེས་རབ་ཙམ་གྱིས་ཇི་ཙམ་དཔྱད་ཀྱང་ཉོན་མོངས་ཟློག་[༨༠]མི་ནུས་ཏེ། ཉོན་མོངས་སྤངས་པའི་ཐར་པ་འཐོབ་པ་ལ་སྟོང་པ་ཉིད་ཀྱི་དོན་ཕྱིན་ཅི་མ་ལོག་པའི་ཡིན་ལུགས་ཕུ་ཐག་ཆོད་པར་རྟོགས་པའི་ལྟ་བ་དེ་དམིགས་པ་ལ་གཡོ་བ་མེད་པའི་ཞི་གནས་ཀྱི་རྟ་ལ་བསྐྱོན་ནས་རྟག་ཆད་ཀྱི་མཐའ་དང་བྲལ་བའི་དབུ་མའི་རིགས་པ་གཏན་ཚིགས་ཆེན་པོ་བཞིའི་མཚོན་རྣོན་པོ་མཐར་འཛིན་གྱི་དམིགས་གཏན་[༨༡] (གཏད་) ཐམས་ཅད་འཇིག་པར་བྱེད་པའི་དེ་ཁོ་ན་ཉིད་ཀྱི་དོན་ལ་ཚུལ་བཞིན་དུ་སྤྱོད་པའི་ཤེས་རབ་ཀྱིས་དེ་ཁོ་ན་ཉིད་རྟོགས་པའི་བློ་གྲོས་རྒྱས་པར་མཛད་དགོས་པའི་ཕྱིར། རྗེ་བླ་མས། རྩེ་གཅིག་བསམ་གཏན་ཙམ་ལ་འཁོར་བ་ཡི། །རྩ་བ་གཅོད་པའི་ནུས་པ་མ་མཐོང་ཞིང་། །ཞི་གནས་ལམ་དང་བྲལ་བའི་ཤེས་རབ་ཀྱིས། །ཇི་ཙམ་དཔྱད་ཀྱང་ཉོན་མོངས་མི་ཟློག་[༨༢]པས། །ཡིན་ལུགས་ཕུ་ཐག་ཆོད་པའི་ཤེས་རབ་དེ། །གཡོ་མེད་ཞི་གནས་རྟ་ལ་བསྐྱོན་ནས་ནི། །མཐའ་བྲལ་དབུ་མའི་རིགས་པའི་མཚོན་རྣོན་གྱིས། །མཐར་འཛིན་དམིགས་གཏད་ཐམས་ཅད་འཇིག་བྱེད་པ། །ཚུལ་བཞིན་སྤྱོད་པའི་ཡངས་པའི་ཤེས་རབ་ཀྱིས། །དེ་ཉིད་རྟོགས་པའི་བློ་གྲོས་རྒྱས་པར་མཛད། །ཅེས་གསུངས།

དེ་ནས་དམིགས་པ་ལ་རྩེ་གཅིག་ཏུ་གཡོ་བ་མེད་པར་འཇོག་པ་ལས་ཞི་གནས་ཀྱི་ཏིང་འཛིན་འགྲུབ་པར་མ་ཟད། རྩེ་གཅིག་པའི་ཏིང་ངེ་འཛིན་ལ་གནས་པའི་ངང་ནས་དེ་ཁོ་ན་ཉིད་ཀྱི་དོན་ལ་ཚུལ་བཞིན་དུ་དཔྱོད་པའི་སོ་སོར་རྟོག་པའི་ཤེས་རབ་ཀྱིས་དཔྱད་པས་ཀྱང་ཡིན་ལུགས་སྟོང་པ་ཉིད་ཀྱི་དོན་ལ་གཡོ་བ་མེད་པར་ཤིན་ཏུ་བརྟན་པའི་ཏིང་

ང་འཛིན་སྐྱེད་[༦༣]པར་མཐོང་ནས་ཞི་ལྷག་ཟུང་དུ་འབྲེལ་བ་བསྒྲུབ་[༦༤]པ་ལ་བརྩོན་པ་ཡ་མཚན་པ་ཡིན་ནོ་སྙམ་དུ་སྨོན་ལམ་གྱི་ཡུལ་དུ་བྱས་ནས་བག་ཆགས་འཇོག་པ་ལ་འབད་དེ། རྗེ་བླ་མས། རྩེ་གཅིག་སྒོམ་[༦༥]པས་ཉིད་འཛིན་འགྲུབ་པར་ནི། །སྨོས་པར་ཅི་འཚལ་ཚུལ་བཞིན་དཔྱོད་པ་ཡི། །སོ་སོར་རྟོག་པ་ཡིས་ཀྱང་ཡིན་ལུགས་ལ། །གཡོ་མེད་ཤིན་ཏུ་བརྟན་པར་གནས་པ་ཡི། །ཧིང་འཛིན་སྐྱེད་[༦༦]པར་མཐོང་ནས་ཞི་ལྷག་གཉིས། །ཟུང་འབྲེལ་སྒྲུབ་[༦༧]ལ་བརྩོན་རྣམས་ཡ་མཚན་ནོ། །ཞེས་གསུངས།

དེ་ལྟ་བུའི་ཞི་ལྷག་ཟུང་འབྲེལ་ལ་མཉམ་པར་བཞག་པའི་ནམ་མཁའ་ལྟ་བུའི་སྤྲོས་པའི་མཐའ་ཐམས་ཅད་དང་བྲལ་བའི་སྟོང་ཉིད་ལ་རྩེ་གཅིག་ཏུ་མཉམ་པར་བཞག་ནས་དེ་ལས་ལངས་པའི་རྗེས་ཐོབ་ཏུ་རང་བཞིན་གྱིས་མ་གྲུབ་ཀྱང་དེ་ལྟར་སྣང་བའི་སྒྱུ་མ་ལྟ་བུའི་སྟོང་པ་ཉིད་བསྒོམས་ནས་སྙིང་རྗེ་དང་བྱང་ཆུབ་ཀྱི་སེམས་ཀྱིས་ཟིན་པའི་ཐབས་ཤེས་ཟུང་དུ་འབྲེལ་བའི་ཉམས་ལེན་གྱིས་རྒྱལ་སྲས་ཀྱི་སྤྱོད་པའི་ཕ་རོལ་ཏུ་འགྲོ་བ་ཤིན་ཏུ་བརྟགས་པར་འོས་ལ། དེ་ལྟར་རྟོགས་ནས་ཐབས་ཤེས་ཡ་བྲལ་བའི་ལམ་ཕྱོགས་རེ་བས་ཆོག་པ་མེད་པར་ཐབས་ཤེས་ཟུང་འབྲེལ་གྱི་ལམ་ལ་སློབ་པ་སྐལ་བཟང་རྣམས་ཀྱི་ལུགས་ཡིན་པས་དེ་ལྟར་འབད་དགོས་ཏེ། རྗེ་བླ་མས། མཉམ་གཞག་[༦༨] (བཞག་) ནམ་མཁའ་ལྟ་བུའི་སྟོང་ཉིད་དང་། །རྗེས་ཐོབ་སྒྱུ་མ་ལྟ་བུའི་སྟོང་པ་གཉིས། །བསྒོམས་པས་[༦༩]ཐབས་ཤེས་ཟུང་དུ་འབྲེལ་བ་ཡིས། །རྒྱལ་སྲས་སྤྱོད་པའི་ཕ་རོལ་འགྲོ་བ་བསྔགས། །དེ་ལྟར་རྟོགས་ནས་ཕྱོགས་རེའི་ལམ་གྱིས་ནི། །ཆོག་པ་མེད་པ་སྐལ་བཟང་རྣམས་ཀྱི་ལུགས། །ཞེས་གསུངས།

དེ་ལྟར་མདོ་སྔགས་ཐུན་མོང་བའི་ལམ་རྣམས་ལ་ལེགས་པར་བསླབས་ནས་གདོན་མི་ཟ་བར་སྔགས་ལ་འཇུག་པར་བྱེད་དགོས་ལ། འཇུག་ཚུལ་ནི་ཐོག་མར་དོ་རྗེ་

སློབ་དཔོན་མཚན་ཉིད་དང་ལྡན་པ་ཞིག་ལས་རྒྱུད་སྡེ་ནས་བཤད་པར་ལྟར་གྱི་དབང་གིས་རྒྱུད་སྨིན་པར་བྱས། དེའི་ཚེ་ཁས་བླངས་པའི་དམ་ཚིག་དང་སྡོམ་པ་ཚུལ་བཞིན་བསྲུངས་ཏེ་རྒྱུད་སྡེ་འོག་མ་གསུམ་ལྟར་ན་མཚན་བཅས་དང་མཚན་མེད་ཀྱི་རྣལ་འབྱོར་ལ་བསླབས་ཤིང་གོང་མ་ལྟར་ན་རིམ་གཉིས་ཀྱི་རྣལ་འབྱོར་ལ་རིམ་ཅན་དུ་བསླབས་པས་མདོ་སྔགས་ཀྱི་ལམ་གྱི་གནད་ཐམས་ཅད་བསྡུས་པའི་ལམ་གྱི་ལུས་ཡོངས་སུ་རྫོགས་པ་ལ་བསླབས་པར་འགྱུར་བས་དལ་འབྱོར་ཐོབ་པ་དོན་ལྡན་དུ་བྱས་པ་ཡིན་ཞིང་། ཚུལ་དེ་ལྟ་བུའི་སྒོ་ནས་རྒྱལ་བའི་བསྟན་པ་རིན་པོ་ཆེ་རང་གཞན་གྱི་རྒྱུད་ལ་སོན་ཨང་།།

རྗེ་བླ་མས་ཀྱང་དེ་ལྟར་དུ་ཐུགས་ཉམས་སུ་བཞེས[༢༠]། བདག་སོགས་རྗེས་འཇུག་རྣམས་ལའང་ཚུལ་དེ་བཞིན་དུ་ཉམས་སུ་ལོང་ཞིག་ཅེས་གདམས་པར་མཛད་པ་ཡིན་སྙམ་དུ་རྗེ་བླ་མ་མདུན་དུ་བསྒོམས་ནས་གསུང་ལྟར་ལྟར་དགྱེས་བཞིན་འདོམས་པར་བསམས་ལ་དངོས་སུ་རང་རང་ཡིད་འཕྲུལ་བའི་སྒོ་ནས་གདོན་པར་བྱའོ། དེ་ལྟར་ཡང་རྗེ་བླ་མས། དེ་ལྟར་རྒྱུ་དང་འབྲས་བུའི་ཐེག་ཆེན་གྱི། །ལམ་མཆོག་གཉིས་ཀར་དགོས་པའི་ཐུན་མོང་ལམ། །ཇི་བཞིན་བསྐྱེད་ནས་མཁས་པའི་དེད་དཔོན་གྱི། །མགོན་ལ་བརྟེན་ནས་རྒྱུད་སྡེའི་རྒྱ་མཚོར[༢༡]ཆེར། །ཞུགས་ནས་ཡོངས་རྫོགས་མན་ངག་བསྟེན[༢༢]པ་དེས། །དལ་འབྱོར་ཐོབ་པ་དོན་དང་ལྡན་པར་བྱས། །རྣལ་འབྱོར་ངས་ཀྱང་ཉམས་ལེན་དེ་ལྟར་བགྱིས། །ཐར་འདོད་ཁྱེད་ཀྱང་དེ་བཞིན་བསྐྱང་འཚལ་ལོ། །རང་གི་ཡིད་ལ་གོམས་པར་བྱ་ཕྱིར་དང་། །སྐལ་བཟང་གཞན་ལའང་ཕན་པར་བྱ་བའི་ཕྱིར། །རྒྱལ་བ་དགྱེས་པའི་ཡོངས་སུ་རྫོགས་པའི་ལམ། །གོ་སླའི་ངག་གིས་བཤད་པའི་དགེ་བ་དེས། །འགྲོ་བ་ཀུན་ཀྱང་རྣམ་དག་ལམ་བཟང་དང་། །འབྲལ་མེད་གྱུར་ཅིག་ཅེས་ནི་སྨོན་ལམ་གདབ[༢༣]། །རྣལ་འབྱོར་ངས་ཀྱང་སྨོན་ལམ་དེ་ལྟར་བཏབ། །ཐར་འདོད་ཁྱེད་ཀྱང་དེ་

བཞིན་འདེབས་འཚལ་ལོ། །ཞེས་གསུང་གདམས་བྱུང་སྙམ་པའི་སྒོ་ནས། དེང་ནས་བརྩམས་ཏེ་ཚེ་རབ་ཀུན་དུ་ ༸ བདག །ཁྱོད་ཞབས་པདྨོ་གུས་པས་མཆོད་པ་དང་། །ཁྱོད་གསུང་ཉན་ཅིང་སྒོ་གསུམ་བྱ་བ་ཀུན། །ཁྱོད་མཉེས་འབའ་ཞིག་སྒྲུབ་པར་བྱིན་གྱིས་རློབས། །ཞེས་སོགས་དང་། ཚེ་རབས་ཀུན་ཏུ་རྒྱལ་བ་ཙོང་ཁ་པས། ཞེས་སོགས་ཀྱིས་བསྔོ་བ་བསམ་པ་ཐག་པ་ནས་བྱའོ།།

ཇོ་བོ་མར་མེ་མཛད་དང་ཙོང་ཁ་པའི། །གདམས་པའི་ཉིང་ཁུ་བྱང་ཆུབ་ལམ་རིམ་གྱི། །ལམ་གྱི་གནད་བསྡུས་མ་ནོར་གདམས་པ་འདིས། །འགྲོ་ཀུན་རྒྱལ་བ་དགྱེས་པའི་ལམ་བགྲོད་ཤོག།

སྐྱེས་བུ་གསུམ་གྱི་ལམ་གྱི་རིམ་པའི་འཁྲིད་བདུད་རྩི་གསེར་གྱི་ཡང་ཞུན་ཞེས་བགྱི་བ་རྗེ་བླ་མའི་ཉམས་མགུར་དང་སྦྱར་ནས་འཇིར་བདེ་བར་བཀོད་པ་འདི་ནི་བསྟན་པའི་གསལ་བྱེད་ཆེན་པོ་ལུགས་འདི་ལ་ཤིན་ཏུ་མོས་ཤིང་དོན་དུ་གཉེར་བ། ཀུན་མཁྱེན་ཆེན་པོ་ཤེས་རབ་དཔལ་བཟང་གི་གདན་ས་བ་ཆེན་པོ་མདོ་ཆོད་ཆོས་རྗེ་ས་གསོལ་བ་ནན་ཆེར་བསྐུལ་བ་ལ་བརྟེན་ནས། ན་ཆོད་ཕྲ་མོ་ནས་རྗེ་བླ་མས་བྱིན་གྱིས་བརླབས་པའི་མཚན་མ་ཐོབ་པ། ཤཱཀྱའི་དགེ་སློང་ཆོས་སྨྲ་བའི་བཙུན་པ་བསོད་ནམས་རྒྱལ་མཆོས་དཔལ་ལྡན་འབྲས་སྤུངས་ཆོས་ཀྱི་སྡེ་ཆེན་པོའི་གཟིམས་ཁང་དགའ་ལྡན་ཕོ་བྲང་གི་ཉི་འོད་རྣམ་པར་འཕྲེལ་བར་སྦྱར་བ་འདིས་ཀྱང་བསྟན་པའི་སྙིང་པོ་ཕྱོགས་དུས་ཀུན་དུ་རྒྱས་པར་བྱེད་ནུས་པར་གྱུར་ཅིག། །།བཀྲ་ཤིས།། །།

ཞུ་སྒྲིག་པའི་མཆན།

ལམ་རིམ་ཉམས་མགུར་གྱི་མཆན།

༡ རྗེ་ཙོང་ཁ་པ། (༡༣༥༧-༡༤༡༩) ཙོང་ཁ་པ་ཆེན་པོའི་བཀའ་འབུམ་ཐོར་བུ་བཞུགས་སོ། ལམ་རིམ་བསྡུས་དོན་(ལམ་རིམ་ཉམས་མགུར།) མཚོ་སྔོན་མི་རིགས་དཔེ་སྐྲུན་ཁང་། ༡༩༨༧ ཤོག་གྲངས། ༡༠༣-༡༠༧ (དེ་རྗེས་བསྡུས་མིང་ལ་ལམ་རིམ་ཉམས་མགུར་ཞེས་འགོད་རྒྱུ།)

༢ དཔལ་དགེ་ལྡན་པའི་ལམ་རིམ་དང་སྔན་བརྒྱུད་ཀྱི་ཆོས་སྐོར་ནང་གཉིས་ནས་ཞེས་འཕོད། རྗེ་ཙོང་ཁ་པ། ལམ་རིམ་ཉམས་མགུར། དཔལ་དགེ་ལྡན་པའི་ལམ་རིམ་དང་སྔན་བརྒྱུད་ཀྱི་ཆོས་སྐོར། བོད་ཀྱི་གཙུག་ལག་ཞིབ་དཔྱོད་ཁང་། ལྡི་ལི། བོད་ཀྱི་གཙུག་ལག་གཅེས་བཏུས་པོད་ཕྲེང་དྲུག་པ། ༢༠༠༥ ཤོགས་གྲངས། ༣-༡༠ བར། (དེ་རྗེས་བསྡུས་མིང་ལ་དཔལ་དགེ་ལྡན་པའི་ལམ་རིམ་དང་སྔན་བརྒྱུད་ཀྱི་ཆོས་སྐོར།)

༣ སྐྱེས་བུ་གསུམ་གྱི་ལམ་གྱི་རིམ་པའི་འཁྲིད་བདུད་རྩི་གསེར་གྱི་ཡང་ཞུན་ནང་སྐྱི་རྒྱུའི་ཞེས་འཕོད།། མ་ཕྱི་འདི་ནི་བོད་ཀྱི་དཔེ་མཛོད་ཁང་གི་ཆོས་དགེ་དགེ་བཤེས་བསོད་ནམས་རིན་ཆེན་ལགས་ཀྱི་གཅེས་ཉར་ཁོངས་ནས་བདག་ལ་མཁོ་སྤྲུབ་གནང་བའི་མ་དཔེ་བྲིས་མ་ཤིན་ཏུ་དག་པ་ཞིག་ཡོད་པ་དེ་ཡིན་ནོ། (འདི་རྗེས་བསྡུས་མིང་ལ་ལམ་རིམ་གསེར་ཞུན་མ་ཞེས་འགོད་རྒྱུ།)

༤ ལམ་རིམ་གསེར་ཞུན་མའི་ནང་སྨྲུང་ཞེས་འཕོད།

༥ དཔལ་དགེ་ལྡན་པའི་ལམ་རིམ་དང་སྔན་བརྒྱུད་ཀྱི་ཆོས་སྐོར་ནང་བསྒྲུབ་ཅེས་འཕོད།

६ ལམ་རིམ་གསེར་ཞུན་མའི་ནང་བྱུས་ཞེས་འབོད་ཅིང་། ཡོངས་གྲགས་སུ་ཁ་འདོན་བྱེད་སྐབས་བྱུས་ཞེས་འདོན།

७ ལམ་རིམ་གསེར་ཞུན་མ་དང་། དེ་ལ་ཁྲུངས་བཅོལ་ནས་བོད་ཀྱི་དཔེ་མཛོད་ཁང་གིས་གློག་གླད་དུ་བཙུག་ནས་གཅེས་ཉར་བྱེད་པ་དང་། དེ་ཉིད་ཤེས་རིག་དཔར་ཁང་གི་དཔར་སྐྲུན་ཞུས་པ་རྣམས་ཀྱི་ནང་སྤྱུན་པ་ཞེས་འབོད།

८ དཔལ་དགེ་ལྡན་པའི་ལམ་རིམ་དང་སྙན་བརྒྱུད་ཀྱི་ཆོས་སྐོར་ནང་གདེངས་ཞེས་འབོད།

९ ལམ་རིམ་གསེར་ཞུན་མའི་ནང་བསྡེན་ཞེས་འབོད།

१० ས་སྤྱོད་ཅེས་ཞོལ་དཔར་མའི་ནང་ཡོད་པ་དཔལ་དགེ་ལྡན་པའི་ལམ་རིམ་དང་སྙན་བརྒྱུད་ཀྱི་ཆོས་སྐོར་གྱི་ཞུ་སྒྲིག་པའི་མཆན་ནང་གསལ།

११ ལམ་རིམ་གསེར་ཞུན་མའི་ནང་ཚང་བ་ཞེས་འབོད།

१२ དཔལ་དགེ་ལྡན་པའི་ལམ་རིམ་དང་སྙན་བརྒྱུད་ཀྱི་ཆོས་སྐོར་ནང་བཏན་དང་། ལམ་རིམ་གསེར་ཞུན་མའི་ནང་བསྡེན་ཞེས་འབོད།

१३ ལམ་རིམ་གསེར་ཞུན་མའི་ནང་ཐེག་ཆེན་ཞེས་འབོད།

१४ ལམ་རིམ་གསེར་ཞུན་མའི་ནང་སྐྱི་རྒྱུའི་ཞེས་འབོད།

१५ དཔལ་དགེ་ལྡན་པའི་ལམ་རིམ་དང་སྙན་བརྒྱུད་ཀྱི་ཆོས་སྐོར་བཟློག་ཅེས་འབོད།

१६ ལམ་རིམ་གསེར་ཞུན་མའི་ནང་གྱུར་ཞེས་འབོད།

१७ ལམ་རིམ་གསེར་ཞུན་མའི་ནང་བརྩམ་ཞེས་འབོད།

१८ ལམ་རིམ་གསེར་ཞུན་མའི་ནང་སྒྱུར་ཞེས་འབོད།

१९ ལམ་རིམ་གསེར་ཞུན་མའི་ནང་དྲུང་ཞེས་འབོད།

२० ལམ་རིམ་གསེར་ཞུན་མའི་ནང་ཟློག་ཅེས་འབོད།

२१ ལམ་རིམ་གསེར་ཞུན་མའི་ནང་སྒོམ་ཞེས་འབོད།

२२ ལམ་རིམ་གསེར་ཞུན་མའི་ནང་སྐྱིད་ཅེས་འབོད།

༢༣ དཔལ་དགེ་ལྡན་པའི་ལམ་རིམ་དང་སྙན་བརྒྱུད་ཀྱི་ཆོས་སྐོར་ནང་མཉམ་བཞག་ཅེས་འཁོད།

༢༤ ལམ་རིམ་གསེར་ཞུན་མའི་ནང་བསྒོམས་པས་ཞེས་འཁོད།

༢༥ ལམ་རིམ་གསེར་ཞུན་མའི་ནང་རྒྱ་མཚོར་ཞེས་འཁོད།

༢༦ ལམ་རིམ་གསེར་ཞུན་མའི་ནང་བསྟེན་ཞེས་འཁོད།

༢༧ ལམ་རིམ་གསེར་ཞུན་མའི་ནང་གདབ་ཅེས་འཁོད།

ལམ་རིམ་གསེར་ཞུན་མའི་མཆན།

༡ རྒྱལ་བ་སྐུ་ཕྲེང་གསུམ་པ་བསོད་ནམས་རྒྱ་མཚོ། (༡༥༤༣-༡༥༨༨) སྐྱེས་བུ་གསུམ་གྱི་ལམ་གྱི་རིམ་པའི་འཁྲིད་བདུད་རྩི་གསེར་གྱི་ཡང་ཞུན་འདི་ཡི་མ་ཕྱི་ནི་བོད་ཀྱི་དཔེ་མཛོད་ཁང་གི་ཆོས་དགེ་དགེ་བཤེས་བསོད་ནམས་རིན་ཆེན་ལགས་ཀྱི་གཅེས་ཉར་ཁྲོངས་ནས་བདག་ལ་མཁོ་སྒྲུབ་གནང་བའི་མ་དཔེ་བྲིས་མ་ཤིན་ཏུ་དག་པ་ཞིག་ཡོད་པ་དེ་ཡིན་ནོ།

༢ རྒྱལ་མཆོག་སྐུ་ཕྲེང་གསུམ་པ་བསོད་ནམས་རྒྱ་མཚོ་དཔལ་བཟང་པོའི་གསུང་འབུམ་ནང་སྐྱེ་དགུ་ཞེས་འཁོད། (སྐུ་སྐོར་ཕྱུག་དཔེ་ཁང་དུ་གཅེས་སྲུང་གནང་བའི་བྲིས་མ་མ་ཕྱི་དེ་ཉིད་བསྐྱར་དུ་པར་སྐྲུན་ཞུས་པ།) བོད་ཀྱི་དཔེ་མཛོད་ཁང་། ཧ་ས། ༢༠༠༠ ཤོག་གྲངས་ ༡-༢༦ བར། (འདི་རྗེས་བསྡུས་མིང་ལ་གསུང་འབུམ་ཞེས་འགོད་རྒྱུ།)

༣ གསུང་འབུམ་དང་ལམ་རིམ་ཉམས་མགུར་ནང་སྐྱེ་དགུའི་ཞེས་འཁོད། རྗེ་ཙོང་ཁ་པ། ལམ་རིམ་ཉམས་མགུར། དཔལ་དགེ་ལྡན་པའི་ལམ་རིམ་དང་སྙན་བརྒྱུད་ཀྱི་ཆོས་སྐོར། བོད་ཀྱི་གཙུག་ལག་ཞིབ་དཔྱོད་ཁང་། ལྡི་ལི། བོད་ཀྱི་གཙུག་ལག་གཅེས་བཏུས་པོད་ཕྲེང་དྲུག་པ། ༢༠༠༥ ལྡི་ལི་གསར་པ། ཤོག་གྲངས། ༣-༡༠ བར། (དེ་རྗེས་བསྡུས་མིང་དཔལ་དགེ་ལྡན་པའི་ལམ་རིམ་དང་སྙན་བརྒྱུད་ཀྱི་ཆོས་སྐོར་ཞེས་འགོད་རྒྱུ།)

༤ གསུང་འབུམ་ནང་བསྒྲུང་དང་། དཔལ་དགེ་ལྡན་པའི་ལམ་རིམ་དང་སྙན་བརྒྱུད་ཀྱི་ཆོས་སྐོར་ནང་བསྒྲུངས་དང་། ཞོལ་དཔར་མའི་ནང་བསྒྲུང་ཡོད་པ་དེའི་ཞུ་སྒྲིག་པའི་མཚན་ནང་གསལ།

༥ གསུང་འབུམ་ནང་དེ་དག་དང་ལྡན་པ་ཞེས་འཁོད།

༦ གསུང་འབུམ་དང་བློ་བཟང་དགོངས་རྒྱན་མུ་ཏིག་འཕྲེང་མཛེས་ནང་བཀོལ་བའི་ཞེས་གསལ། བློ་བཟང་དགོངས་རྒྱན་མུ་ཏིག་འཕྲེང་མཛེས། འབྲས་བློ་གླིང་ཤེས་ཡོན་ལྷན་ཚོགས། མོན་སྒོ། ༡༩༩༧ དེབ་འཕྲེང་། ༣༤ ཤོག་གྲངས། ༡-༣༡ (འདི་རྗེས་བསྡུས་མིང་བློ་བཟང་དགོངས་རྒྱན་ཞེས་འགོད་རྒྱུ།)

༧ གསུང་འབུམ་ནང་བརྟེགས་ཞེས་འཁོད།

༨ གསུང་འབུམ་དང་བློ་བཟང་དགོངས་རྒྱན་དུ་ཡན་ལག་བདུན་པ་ཞེས་འཁོད།

༩ བློ་བཟང་དགོངས་རྒྱན་དུ་དེ་ལ་ནི་ཞེས་འཁོད།

༡༠ འདི་ནི་རང་བྱུང་བཅོམ་ལྡན་འདས། །གཅིག་པུ་བདག་ཉིད་ཆེ་བའི་ལྷ། །མན་ངག་རྣམས་ནི་རབ་སྟེར་བས། །རྡོ་རྗེ་སློབ་དཔོན་དེ་བས་ལྷག །ཅེས་མགོན་པོ་ཀླུ་སྒྲུབ་ཀྱི་རྫོགས་རིམ་པ་ལྔའི་རིམ་པ་བཞི་པའི་ནང་ཚིགས་བཅད་འདི་གསལ། སྡེ་གེ། རྒྱུད་ངི། ཤོག་གྲངས། ༡༠༦བ༧།

༡༡ གསུང་འབུམ་ནང་དགེན་པ་ཞེས་འཁོད།

༡༢ གསུང་འབུམ་ནང་འཆུགས་པ་ཞིག་ཞེས་འཁོད།

༡༣ གསུང་འབུམ་ནང་གདམ་ངམ་ཞེས་འཁོད།

༡༤ གསུང་འབུམ་ནང་བདུད་དུ་ཞེས་འཁོད།

༡༥ གསུང་འབུམ་ནངསྐྱོན་གང་ལ་ཡོད་ཅེས་འཁོད།

༡༦ དཔལ་དགེ་ལྡན་པའི་ལམ་རིམ་དང་སྙན་བརྒྱུད་ཀྱི་ཆོས་སྐོར་དང་གསུང་འབུམ་ནང་བསྒྲུབ་ཞེས་འཁོད།

༡༧ ལམ་རིམ་ཉམས་མགུར་ནང་བགྱིས་ཅེས་འཁོད། འོན་ཀྱང་ཡོངས་གྲགས་སུ་ཁ་འདོན་བྱེད་སྐབས་བྱས་ཞེས་འདོན།

༡༨ གསུང་འབུམ་ནང་སྨྲུན་པ་ཞེས་འཁོད།

༡༩ གསུང་འབུམ་ནང་ལྡོག་ཅེས་འཁོད།

༢༠ ལམ་རིམ་ཉམས་མགུར་དང་གསུང་འབུམ་ནང་སྨྲུན་པ་ཞེས་འཁོད།

༢༡ གསུང་འབུམ་ནང་སྲིད་པའི་བདེ་ལ་ཞེས་འཁོད།

༢༢ གསུང་འབུམ་ནང་ལྡོག་ཅེས་འཁོད།

༢༣ གསུང་འབུམ་ནང་ཕུན་ཚོགས་ལ་ཞེས་འཁོད།

༢༤ གསུང་འབུམ་ནང་གཏོགས་ཞེས་འཁོད།

༢༥ བློ་བཟང་དགོངས་རྒྱན་ནང་གང་ཅམ་ན་ཞེས་འཁོད།

༢༦ གསུང་འབུམ་ནང་གར་སོང་ཞེས་འཁོད།

༢༧ བློ་བཟང་དགོངས་རྒྱན་དང་གསུང་འབུམ་ནང་དེ་རིང་ཞེས་འཁོད།

༢༨ གསུང་འབུམ་ནང་བཅད་ཅེས་འཁོད།

༢༩ བློ་བཟང་དགོངས་རྒྱན་དུ་སེར་པོ་ཞེས་འཁོད།

༣༠ གསུང་འབུམ་ནང་སྐྱབས་སུ་སོང་ནས་ཞེས་འཁོད།

༣༡ རི་དང་ནགས་བཅས་ས་འདི་གས་གྱུར་ཅིང་། །རྒྱ་མཚོའི་ཆུ་དག་དེ་བཞིན་གས་གྱུར་ལ། །ཟླ་བ་ཉི་མ་ས་ལ་ལྷུང་གྱུར་ཀྱང་། རྒྱལ་བས་བཤད་པ་རྣམ་པ་གཞན་མི་འགྱུར་ཞེས་ཏིང་ངེ་འཛིན་རྒྱལ་པོའི་མདོའི་ནང་ཚིགས་བཅད་འདི་གསལ། སྡེ་གེ། མདོ་ད། ཤོགས་གྲངས། ༥༡ན༢

༣༢ མི་དགེ་བ་ལས་སྡུག་བསྔལ་འབྱུང་། །དེ་ལས་ཇི་ལྟར་ངེས་ཐར་ཞེས། ཉིན་མཚན་རྟག་ཏུ་བདག་གིས་ནི། །འདི་ཉིད་འབའ་ཞིག་བསམ་པའི་རིགས། ཅེས་བྱང་ཆུབ་སེམས་དཔའི་སྤྱོད་པ་ལ་འཇུག་པའི་ནང་གསལ། སྡེ་གེ། ཤོག་གྲངས། ༦བ༡

༣༣ དགེ་བའི་ཕྱོགས་ནི་ཐམས་ཅད་ཀྱི། རྩ་བ་མོས་པར་ཐུབ་པས་གསུངས། །དེའི་ཡང་རྩ་བ་རྟག་ཏུ་ནི། །རྣམ་སྨིན་འབྲས་བུ་བསྒོམས་པས་སོ། ཞེས་བྱང་ཆུབ་སེམས་དཔའི་སྤྱོད་པ་ལ་འཇུག་པ། སྡེ་གེ། ཤོག་གྲངས། ༢༡བ༤

༣༤ རྒྱལ་པོའི་དྲུང་དུ་ཕྱིན་པའི་ལེའུ། འཕགས་པ་བྱང་ཆུབ་སེམས་དཔའི་སྤྱོད་ཡུལ་གྱི་ཐབས་ཀྱི་ཡུལ་ལ་རྣམ་པར་འཕྲུལ་བ་བསྟན་པ་ཞེས་བྱ་བ་ཐེག་པ་ཆེན་པོའི་མདོ། སྡེ་གེ། ཤོག་གྲངས། ༡༠༡ན༣

༣༥ དཔལ་དགེ་ལྡན་པའི་ལམ་རིམ་དང་སྙན་བརྒྱུད་ཀྱི་ཆོས་སྐོར་ནང་གདེངས་ཅེས་འཁོད།

༣༦ དཔལ་དགེ་ལྡན་པའི་ལམ་རིམ་དང་སྙན་བརྒྱུད་ཀྱི་ཆོས་སྐོར་ནང་བརྟན་ཞེས་འཁོད།

༣༧ གསུང་འབུམ་ནང་སེམས་ཅན་གཞན་ལ་ཞེས་འཁོད།

༣༨ བློ་བཟང་དགོངས་རྒྱན་དང་གསུང་འབུམ་ནང་བསྐྱེན་ཞེས་འཁོད།

༣༩ ས་ཕྱོད་ཅེས་ཞོལ་དཔར་མའི་ནང་ཡོད་པ་དཔལ་དགེ་ལྡན་པའི་ལམ་རིམ་དང་སྙན་བརྒྱུད་ཀྱི་ཆོས་སྐོར་གྱི་ཞུ་སྒྲིག་པའི་མཆན་ནང་གསལ།

༤༠ དཔལ་དགེ་ལྡན་པའི་ལམ་རིམ་དང་སྙན་བརྒྱུད་ཀྱི་ཆོས་སྐོར་ནང་ཚང་བར་ཞེས་འཁོད།

༤༡ གསུང་འབུམ་ནང་འགྲོ་ན་ནི་ཞེས་འཁོད།

༤༢ བློ་བཟང་དགོངས་རྒྱན་ནང་ཚད་པས་ཞེས་འཁོད།

༤༣ གསུང་འབུམ་ནང་ཚོང་ཟོང་ཞེས་འཁོད།

༤༤ དཔལ་དགེ་ལྡན་པའི་ལམ་རིམ་དང་སྙན་བརྒྱུད་ཀྱི་ཆོས་སྐོར་ནང་བརྟན་ཞེས་འཁོད། སྐུ་འབུམ་དཔར་མའི་ནང་བརྟེན་ཞེས་ཡོད་པ་དེའི་ཞུ་སྒྲིག་པའི་མཆན་ནང་གསལ།

༤༥ གསུང་འབུམ་ནང་ཉེ་རིང་བར་མར་ཕྱེ་ནས་ཞེས་འཁོད།

༤༦ གསུང་འབུམ་ནང་སེམས་ཅན་རྣམས་ལའང་སེམས་མཉམ་པར་བྱ་ཞེས་འཁོད།

༤༧ གསུང་འབུམ་ནང་བློས་མི་སྤོང་བ་ཞེས་འཁོད།

༤༨ བློ་བཟང་དགོངས་རྒྱན་དང་གསུང་འབུམ་ནང་བཞད་ཅེས་འཁོད།

༤༩ བློ་བཟང་དགོངས་རྒྱན་དང་གསུང་འབུམ་ནང་བརྗོད་ཅེས་འཁོད།

༥༠ དཔལ་དགེ་ལྡན་པའི་ལམ་རིམ་དང་སྙན་བརྒྱུད་ཀྱི་ཆོས་སྐོར་དང་བློ་བཟང་དགོངས་རྒྱན་དུ་ཐེག་མཆོག་ཅེས་འཁོད།

༥༡ དཔལ་དགེ་ལྡན་པའི་ལམ་རིམ་དང་སྙན་བརྒྱུད་ཀྱི་ཆོས་སྐོར་དང་གསུང་འབུམ་ནང་སྐྱེ་དགུའི་ཞེས་འཁོད།

༥༢ དཔལ་དགེ་ལྡན་པའི་ལམ་རིམ་དང་སྙན་བརྒྱུད་ཀྱི་ཆོས་སྐོར་དང་གསུང་འབུམ་ནང་བསྒྲུང་ཞེས་འཁོད།

༥༣ གསུང་འབུམ་ནང་ཆོས་ལ་ངེས་སེམས་ཀྱི་བཟོད་པ་སྟེ་ཞེས་འཁོད།

༥༤ དཔལ་དགེ་ལྡན་པའི་ལམ་རིམ་དང་སྙན་བརྒྱུད་ཀྱི་ཆོས་སྐོར་ནང་མི་བཟློག་ཅེས་འཁོད།

༥༥ དཔལ་དགེ་ལྡན་པའི་ལམ་རིམ་དང་སྙན་བརྒྱུད་ཀྱི་ཆོས་སྐོར་དང་གསུང་འབུམ་ནང་འགྱུར་ཞེས་འཁོད།

༥༦ དཔལ་དགེ་ལྡན་པའི་ལམ་རིམ་དང་སྙན་བརྒྱུད་ཀྱི་ཆོས་སྐོར་དང་གསུང་འབུམ་ནང་བརྩམས་ཞེས་འཁོད།

༥༧ དཔལ་དགེ་ལྡན་པའི་ལམ་རིམ་དང་སྙན་བརྒྱུད་ཀྱི་ཆོས་སྐོར་ནང་བསྒྱུར་ཞེས་འཁོད།

༥༨ དཔལ་དགེ་ལྡན་པའི་ལམ་རིམ་དང་སྙན་བརྒྱུད་ཀྱི་ཆོས་སྐོར་དང་གསུང་འབུམ་ནང་དྲུངས་ཞེས་འཁོད།

༥༩ གསུང་འབུམ་ནང་དེ་ནས་ཕར་ཕྱིན་དྲུག་ཅེས་འཁོད།

༦༠ གསུང་འབུམ་ནང་བཟློག་ཅེས་འཁོད།

༦༡ བློ་བཟང་དགོངས་རྒྱན་དང་གསུང་འབུམ་ནང་དམིགས་གཏད་ཅེས་འཁོད།

༦༢ དཔལ་དགེ་ལྡན་པའི་ལམ་རིམ་དང་སྙན་བརྒྱུད་ཀྱི་ཆོས་སྐོར་ནང་མི་ལྡོག་ཅེས་དང་གསུང་འབུམ་ནང་མི་བཟློག་ཅེས་འཁོད།

༦༣ གསུང་འབུམ་ནང་བསྐྱེད་ཅེས་འཁོད།

༦༤ གསུང་འབུམ་ནང་བསླུབ་ཅེས་འཕོད།

༦༥ དཔལ་དགེ་ལྡན་པའི་ལམ་རིམ་དང་སྙན་བརྒྱུད་ཀྱི་ཆོས་སྐོར་ནང་གོམས་ཞེས་དང་། གསུང་འབུམ་ནང་བསྒོམས་ཞེས་འཕོད།

༦༦ དཔལ་དགེ་ལྡན་པའི་ལམ་རིམ་དང་སྙན་བརྒྱུད་ཀྱི་ཆོས་སྐོར་དང་གསུང་འབུམ་ནང་བསྐྱེད་ཅེས་འཕོད།

༦༧ གསུང་འབུམ་ནང་བསླུབ་ཅེས་འཕོད།

༦༨ དཔལ་དགེ་ལྡན་པའི་ལམ་རིམ་དང་སྙན་བརྒྱུད་ཀྱི་ཆོས་སྐོར་ནང་བཞག་ཅེས་འཕོད།

༦༩ དཔལ་དགེ་ལྡན་པའི་ལམ་རིམ་དང་སྙན་བརྒྱུད་ཀྱི་ཆོས་སྐོར་ནང་བསྒོམས་ནས་ཞེས་འཕོད།

༧༠ གསུང་འབུམ་ནང་རྗེ་བླ་མས་ཀྱང་ཐུགས་དེ་ལྟར་དུ་ཉམས་སུ་བཞེས་ཞེས་འཕོད།

༧༡ དཔལ་དགེ་ལྡན་པའི་ལམ་རིམ་དང་སྙན་བརྒྱུད་ཀྱི་ཆོས་སྐོར་དང་གསུང་འབུམ་ནང་རྒྱ་མཚོ་ཞེས་འཕོད།

༧༢ དཔལ་དགེ་ལྡན་པའི་ལམ་རིམ་དང་སྙན་བརྒྱུད་ཀྱི་ཆོས་སྐོར་ནང་བརྟེན་ཞེས་འཕོད་ཅིང་བསྟེན་ཞེས་ཞོལ་དཔར་མའི་ནང་ཡོད་པ་དེའི་ཞུ་སྒྲིག་པའི་མཆན་ནང་གསལ།

༧༣ དཔལ་དགེ་ལྡན་པའི་ལམ་རིམ་དང་སྙན་བརྒྱུད་ཀྱི་ཆོས་སྐོར་ནང་འདི་བས་ཞེས་འཕོད།

༧༤ གསུང་འབུམ་ནང་ཀུན་ཏུ་ཞེས་འཕོད།

ཞུ་སྒྲིག་པའི་ཁུངས་བཙལ་གྱི་ཡིག་ཆ་ཁག

སྟོན་པ་ཤཱཀྱ་ཐུབ་པ། ཏིང་ངེ་འཛིན་རྒྱལ་པོའི་མདོ། མདོ་དེ། སྡེ་དགེ།

མགོན་པོ་ཀླུ་སྒྲུབ། རྫོགས་རིམ་རིམ་ལྔ་། རྒྱུད་དེ་། སྡེ་དགེ།

རྗེ་ཙོང་ཁ་པ་བློ་བཟང་གྲགས་པ། (༡༣༥༧-༡༤༡༩) ལམ་རིམ་བསྡུས་དོན་ནམ་ལམ་རིམ་ཉམས་མགུར། མཚོ་སྔོན་མི་རིགས་དཔེ་སྐྲུན་ཁང་། ༡༩༨༧ ཤོག་གྲངས། ༡༠༣-༡༠༧

——— ལམ་རིམ་ཉམས་མགུར། དཔལ་ལྡན་དགེ་ལྡན་པའི་ལམ་རིམ་དང་སྙན་བརྒྱུད་ཀྱི་ཆོས་སྐོར། བོད་ཀྱི་གཙུག་ལག་ཞིབ་དཔྱོད་ཁང་། ལྡི་ལི། བོད་ཀྱི་གཙུག་ལག་གཅེས་བཏུས་པོད་ཕྲེང་དྲུག་པ། ༢༠༠༥ ཤོགས་གྲངས། ༢-༡༠ བར།

རྒྱལ་བ་སྐུ་འཕྲེང་གསུམ་པ་བསོད་ནམས་རྒྱ་མཚོ། (༡༥༤༣-༡༥༨༨) སྐྱེས་བུ་གསུམ་གྱི་ལམ་གྱི་རིམ་པའི་འཁྲིད་བདུད་རྩི་གསེར་གྱི་ཡང་ཞུན། བོད་ཀྱི་དཔེ་མཛོད་ཁང་གི་དགེ་བཤེས་བསོད་ནམས་རིན་ཆེན་ལགས་ཀྱི་མ་དཔེ་བྲིས་མ།

——— བློ་གསལ་གླིང་ཤེས་ཡོན་ལྷན་ཚོགས། བློ་བཟང་དགོངས་རྒྱན་མུ་ཏིག་འཕྲེང་མཛེས་དེབ་ཕྲེང་ཉི་ཤུ་རྩ་བཞི། ༡༩༩༧ ཤོག་གྲངས། ༡-༣༡

——— རྒྱལ་མཆོག་སྐུ་ཕྲེང་གསུམ་པ་བསོད་ནམས་རྒྱ་མཚོ་དཔལ་བཟང་པོའི་གསུང་འབུམ། (སྐུ་སྒེར་ཕྱག་དཔེ་ཁང་དུ་གཅེས་སྲུང་གནང་བའི་བྲིས་མ་མ་ཕྱི་དེ་ཉིད་བསྐྱར་དུ་པར་སྐྲུན་ཞུས་པ།) བོད་ཀྱི་དཔེ་མཛོད་ཁང་། ༢༠༠༠

——— བོད་ཀྱི་དཔེ་མཛོད་ཁང་ནས་གློག་ཀླད་དུ་བཙུག་ནས་ཕྱག་དཔེ་རུ་གཅེས་ཉར་བྱས་པ། ད་ས། ༡༩༩༥

——— ཤེས་རིག་དཔར་ཁང་། ད་ས། ༡༩༩༦

ཡོངས་འཛིན་ཡེ་ཤེས་རྒྱལ་མཚན། (༡༧༡༣-༡༧༩༣) ལམ་རིམ་བླ་མ་བརྒྱུད་པའི་རྣམ་ཐར། བོད་ལྗོངས་མི་དམངས་དཔེ་སྐྲུན་ཁང་། ལྷ་ས། ༡༩༩༠

དུང་དཀར་བློ་བཟང་འཕྲིན་ལས། (༡༩༢༥-༡༩༩༧) དུང་དཀར་ཚིག་མཛོད། ཤེས་རིག་དཔར་ཁང་། རྡ་ས། ༢༠༠༥

——— ལོ་ཆིགས་དྭངས་ཤེལ་མེ་ལོང་། དུང་དཀར་ཚིག་མཛོད། ཤེས་རིག་དཔར་ཁང་། རྡ་ས། ༢༠༠༥

ཡཱ་ཏན་ཀྲུང་། པཎ་ཆེན་སྐུ་ཕྲེང་རིམ་བྱོན་གྱི་མཛད་རྣམ། (བློ་བཟང་ཕུན་ཚོགས་དང་རྟ་མགྲིན་འབྲུག་གྲགས་ཀྱིས་བོད་ཡིག་ཏུ་བསྒྱུར།) བོད་ལྗོངས་མི་དམངས་དཔེ་སྐྲུན་ཁང་། ལྷ་ས། ༡༩༩༢